A Practice of Loss

Christina Houen's first memoir, *This Place You Know*, entwines the story of her childhood with her mother's story, set on a small sheep farm in outback New South Wales. Love of place binds mother and daughter, who struggle to keep the farm going against all odds after Anna's father takes off with another woman.

A Practice of Loss reads like a novel, but this is real life with cruel twists.
   Marian Matta, author of *Life, Bound* (Midnight Sun Press)

An evocative and poignant story, heartbreaking at times.
   Jacqui Hodder, author of *The Sentinel* (Blue Wren Press)

Despite the darkness of the theme, the writing is exquisite and compelling to the very end. I could not put it down.

Christina Marigold Houen

A Practice of Loss

Memoir of an abandoning mother

Author's note: the names of people who are mentioned in this memoir have been changed to protect their privacy.

A Practice of Loss: Memoir of an abandoning mother
ISBN 978 1 76109 200 8
Copyright © text Christina Houen 2021

First published 2021 by
GINNINDERRA PRESS
PO Box 3461 Port Adelaide 5015
www.ginninderrapress.com.au

For my three daughters, with love unending.

Prologue

Marriage mortgaged me and bankrupted me. My husband took title of my life. When I attempted to claim it back, he forced me to pay a huge penalty that kept me shackled. Now, aged eighty, I look back on a life lived backwards for many years. I learned to love unconditionally and to live through grief and regret. Until, at last, I recognised the gifts that had been given when my life fell apart.

One

I'm looking forward to tonight. I'll have the bed to myself, such a luxury. Robert is off to another conference, in the Lake District this time. He's upstairs packing the last things. He'll be placing his best shirt that has been ironed and folded for him on the top layer of his suitcase, checking his briefcase for the notes he needs for the paper he'll give. He's a meticulous packer, but he expects me to have his clothes all laid out ready for him. He's never ironed a shirt in his life. He asks me to do it, not our housekeeper – 'You do a better job of the collar and the sleeves!'

His taste in clothes has changed since we met twelve years ago. He used to wear loud shirts, checks and stripes, ties that didn't match. In the first few years, before we had children, I went shopping with him and gently suggested he try better quality fabrics, more muted colours. Now, he does his own shopping, mostly when he's away, but sometimes he brings home a dud, like a loud American suit in plaid with bell bottom trousers, which made his figure look shorter and fatter.

'Tapered legs are in fashion now, Robert,' I said, 'and I think they will suit you much better.'

When he was away last time, I took the plaid outfit to the op shop and bought a pair of casual trousers in Harris tweed, a muted herringbone pattern of browns and greys.

I hear his muffled footsteps on the staircase. We had it covered in a thick, plushy burgundy red carpet: thick to absorb the sound, burgundy because I love rich dark colours. When he reaches the hallway, he puts his suitcase and briefcase down by the hallstand. He's wearing the Harris tweed with a cream shirt and his brown leather jacket, which I bought as a present for his last birthday. I marked O level English papers to pay for it all through December.

He pats his jacket and turns to me. 'How do I look?' He pulls out his wallet and takes out some notes. 'Here's housekeeping for the next week. Should see you through till I get back.'

'Thank you. You look very smart. Lucky you, going to the Lakes! I'd love to go back there.' We went there, pulling a caravan, when Caitlin was a baby and Sophia was three, but only stayed one night. When Robert goes on a trip, he always wants to push on to the next destination. So that trip was one day at the Lakes, on to Inverness, around the coast of the Highlands, then back to Oban on the west coast, through Glasgow, on through the Midlands and home. All in a week.

'Bob's picking me up in about ten minutes,' he says, checking his watch. 'Remember to log in every day while I'm away and stay logged on for a couple of hours at least, even if you've done all the coding, so I can claim for your time. Come and I'll show you what I want you to do.'

He walks into the playroom and I follow him. Sophia and Caitlin are playing mothers and fathers with Penelope as their baby. They have a playhouse, what the English call a Wendy house, after the one that was built for Wendy Darling in Peter Pan. I got our housekeeper's husband to make it for their last Christmas. They can use it as a shop or a house, and I've furnished it with pots and pans, small wooden furniture, and a doll's cot. They're absorbed in their game, and don't notice us standing at the console.

Robert pats a pile of coding paper on the desk. 'I've written out some coding here for you. It's all straightforward stuff you've done before.'

He brought a console home from the lab when Sophia was a toddler and installed it in the bedroom of the semi-detached house on the Atomic Energy Estate in Abingdon – our first home in England. He taught me how to code data into it and began logging me in each day so I could earn some housekeeping money. Now, at least, it's not in the bedroom.

'OK,' I say, as he sits down in the office chair and riffles through the pages, checking them. I walk over to the girls. 'Come, darlings, come and say goodbye to Daddy. He's going away for a few days.'

Sophia and Caitlin run over to him, and I pick Penelope up and place her on his knee.

He hugs and kisses her and then scoops the other two to his chest, folding them all in a bear hug. 'Be good for Mummy, and I'll be back soon.'

'How long will you be away, Daddy?' says Sophia.

'Just a few days. I'll be back before next weekend.' He stands and kisses me.

His moustache scratches my lips, which get chapped when the weather's dry; he must have trimmed it short this morning, just when it was softening up. I press my lips together and moisten them.

'I'll ring you when I get there. Walk out to the road with me.'

We set off, Penelope in his arms, Sophia and Caitlin running ahead. Saturday afternoon in late October, a lovely English autumn day in Oxfordshire. Autumn is my favourite time of year here, when the sun shines slantwise across the fields, the leaves are turning gold and amber on the horse chestnut trees at the front of our garden, and the blackberries are ripening in the hedgerows. A mist rises from the fields in the mornings and hovers till midday sometimes.

A soft breeze blows off the Berkshire Downs to the south, lifting Robert's cowlick. The cowlick is the bane of his life. He tries to flatten it and spread it over his forehead with hairspray, so it doesn't lift and show his balding patches, but it has a glassy, unnatural look. He pats it down and forges ahead, anxious to be at the roadside waiting when Bob arrives. Bob works at the laboratory with him and they car pool.

The girls are playing under the horse chestnut trees, picking up conkers and throwing them at each other. An old blue Morris Oxford pulls up, and Robert opens the passenger door and calls them over for a last hug.

He turns to me. 'Bye, darling. Look after them for me.' A hasty scratchy kiss and he's in, door shut, and they drive away.

Seeing him off and welcoming him home, comings and goings, punctuate our lives. Even when he's not away, he spends more time at work than he does at home. The most time we spend together is when we're asleep. Mostly, I'm happy when he's away. The worst time was when Penelope was a baby, about three months old. He was in the States for about three weeks, and the three girls got chickenpox, one after the other. Penelope was the sickest, with a high fever, crying all the time. I got little sleep, just paced the floor, nursing her, using damp cloths, tepid baths and doses of aspirin to soothe her and bring her fever down. Just me and three sick little girls. I've never felt so alone. The older two weren't so sick, but they were miserable and uncomfortable and quarrelled a lot. I was glad when he came home. He's good at holding them and comforting them, distracting them with little games and stories.

I turn back to the house, holding Penelope's hand as she trots behind Sophia and Caitlin, who are keen to get back to their game. I sit with Penelope on the couch, pulling up my jumper to give her my breast. She's twenty months old, and still enjoys feeding from me during the day, but sleeps through the night now. I relax into the brocaded cushions, rubbing my cheek on the fine golden floss of her baby curls.

I feel at home here, though I am not from English soil. From outback New South Wales, to school in the Tablelands, to Sydney, I've had many homes. After Robert and I got married, we lived in his upstairs flat on the noisy, smelly, grimy main road that linked the inner city with the outer western suburbs. It was close to Sydney University, where we both worked. Then we moved to an old brown block of flats on the harbour in Kirribilli, a much pleasanter setting, and lived there until I had Sophia. When she was three months old, we came to England. Once we settled in, I came to love the life here, and feel more at home than I have since I was a child in the outback.

When Robert's not here, I don't feel lonely, I feel safe. The house settles around us, holding us, its ancient wattle and daub walls quietly humming to each other of past births and deaths, comings and goings, and the voices of children. The tiles on the roof creak and murmur when they warm up on sunny days after frosty nights. I dream of what the house was like back in the sixteenth century, when it was built. They would have had cows in the barn and chooks in the attic. I wonder if the yew trees in the front garden were planted then. They look ancient, ragged, stiff with age, like churchyard watchers over the dead. Sometimes, the girls play in the front garden, but I have to watch them, because the yew berries are very poisonous. Once, Sophia rushed in and told me Caitlin had swallowed some. I got some ipecac from the bathroom cupboard and gave her half a teaspoonful. As I waited anxiously, wondering if I should take her to hospital, she vomited up some berry-stained mucus, and I gave her warm milk to drink.

Robert is hardly ever here when these crises happen, and I'm used to coping. I would love to feel settled here, never to leave. But I know he's planning his next move. His ambition never sleeps, and he's always several steps ahead of me. He doesn't tell me much, but I know that once he's made his name in computer science with the system he's setting up, he'll be off to a more demanding and important job. When that happens, I wish it could be somewhere in England or Scotland. Perhaps it's my Celtic ancestry.

Penelope's mouth stops sucking and her breathing slows down, her little hands twitching as she falls asleep. Outside, the wind has littered the grass with golden pointed leaves from the horse chestnut trees. There is a chill in the air, a musky, sweet smell of bracken and country hedgerows, with base notes of animal manure and rotting hay from the farmyard next door. I look across at the inglenook fireplace, wishing I could persuade Robert to unseal the chimney and get it cleaned so we can light a fire in the huge grate. The cockney family we bought the house from had rebuilt the fireplace from hand-carved Cotswold stone, then sealed it off and put a television in there. Robert likes this, because it's functional. Like the bar they built in the corner leading into the 'drawing room', which we don't use because it is dark and musty, with peeling wallpaper and dingy curtains. The bar is large and imposing, shaped from stone pieces of various sizes, and Robert loves it and shows it off to friends when they come. He keeps his collection of duty-free liqueurs there.

We came to England from Australia seven years ago so he could pursue his career as a computer scientist. His first love is computers. He developed a passion for them when he was doing his PhD in Sydney in physics. His supervisor was a nuclear physicist, running a big program tracking cosmic radiation emitted by stars through an array of machinery on the roof of the Physics department. Robert's task was to feed the data into the computer and set up systems to analyse it. This was back in the late 1950s when SILLIAC, the computer he worked on, was only the second analogue computer in the world. He worshipped it, and spent many late-night hours feeding it with data and supervising the technicians. The second date we had, he took me down into the bowels of the Physics department to show it to me. I saw an overgrown metal filing cabinet. It filled a whole room. I stared at it, mesmerised by its monotonous hum and the red and green lights flashing on and off. Technicians moved to and fro, speaking to each other in low voices, always returning to the machine, ministering to it. It was a modern-day minotaur at the centre of an electronic labyrinth.

How did I get absorbed into this surreal world where machinery rules, where data and abstruse theories of the universe, the Big Bang, artificial intelligence, quantum physics, the nature of matter, are more important than the world of the imagination, poetry, writing, nature, people, relationships, love?

I find it alien, as I find Robert alien. At first, I was attracted to him because he was intelligent, ambitious, clever, different from the lost lovely boys I'd connected with and disconnected from, tearing their heart or mine. He loved partying and came to life when he danced. He seemed to know where he was going, and I didn't know what I wanted to do with my life. So far, I'd drifted from school to uni, studying the subjects I liked and was good at, but I had no ambition to be an academic. I wanted to escape from my mother to a different world where she could not hold sway. She'd dominated my life since I was seven, when my father left, never to return to his family.

Robert is the architect of our domestic life, and we live here on his terms, enfolded by a soft English climate, layers of history and culture, many voices, many accents. In this world, I feel welcome, almost known. His work provides a domestic shelter where I strive to make a beautiful, homely space for us, for our little daughters, and a hospitable space for our friends. That feels real. But we are held afloat by Robert's bubble of data, an inhuman world where electronic signals matter more than humans, red light or green light, on-off, on-off, and it is all driven by money and ego and the race to be first to solve the problems of remote electronic connection, to be a pioneer and a leader of this esoteric knowledge that is destined to run the world.

Evening falls and I call the girls in from the playroom. 'Nearly teatime, darlings. Do you want to watch cartoons while I get tea?'

'Yes, yes,' they clamour.

'Just half an hour.' I sit Penelope down with them on cushions on the floor and turn the TV on.

Their favourite meal is scrambled eggs, peas and potato. Their plates are quickly emptied. They help me take the dishes into the kitchen, then I run a bath for them. They love splashing together, bigger sisters either end, Penelope in the middle. I can safely leave her with them now. Down in the playroom, I pick up their toys and stack the little pots and pans and utensils on the shelves in the Wendy house.

> I wish I had a darling house
> The littlest ever seen,
> With funny little red walls
> And roof of mossy green,

I chant, remembering when I took them to see *Peter Pan* at the cinema in Wantage. Robert came too; he loves fantasy movies, becomes a little boy again, like their big brother. He is happiest when he is playing with them or watching cartoons and stories with them. He once said to me, 'If we're at a party together and you see me across the room, I want you to see I'm just a little boy, wanting to be loved.' He loves parties too, talking, drinking, dancing. I think it was the little boy I fell in love with when we first met at a party…his enthusiasm, *joie de vivre*, his bright, sparkling energy. But as he's become more successful, that little boy has been buried in layers of work, ambition and determination.

He and I lost touch years ago… I'm not sure when, perhaps when we lived in the States for a few months while he was on sabbatical. We became friends with an Australian couple. Malcolm was in the same department as Robert, and Marie was an at-home mum like me. Malcolm had a crush on me, and Robert was very jealous. I could see he and Marie were attracted to each other too. The two Ms talked to us about swinging. We decided it was too risky. One of us might fall in love with the other person.

I got pregnant. It was unplanned, but I think Robert's desire for me was fanned by jealousy. He wanted a boy. I wanted another girl. I didn't feel ready to have a boy child.

He suggested I leave early so I could spend some time in Sydney with my family. He stayed on with Malcolm and Marie for a month. When he joined me, we went up to Mackay to visit his parents. In bed the first night we were there, he told me he and Marie had fallen in love.

'I thought it was just a fling at first,' he said, as we lay under the mosquito net, sweating in the tropical night. 'She'd come to my bed, we'd make love, then she would go back to Malcolm and tell him what we'd done.'

I was furious, and wondered if he'd done it, at least to start with, to get back at me for the flirtation with Malcolm. Five months pregnant, I felt despairing about our marriage. When we returned to England, I tried to persuade him to have marriage counselling with me, but he refused, and buried himself in his work. I had one session with a psychiatrist on the National Health, with two students sitting in; I spent the hour defending Robert for not being there.

I resigned myself to an empty relationship that holds me in a world I don't belong in. My love for my daughters is what keeps me here. When Penelope arrived, I came back to life, and threw myself into mothering my three little girls and making the best of my England.

Without Robert, after all, I would not have come here and discovered the joys of this multilayered, ancient culture and rich countryside. I have much to thank him for – three beautiful daughters, a spacious period house in a quiet village surrounded by fields and Downs, a comfortable way of life, and the privilege of being a home mum.

The console's lights are flashing; I forgot to turn it off. Robert's machine. Robert's house. Robert's world. I am here on his terms. I turn it off and go upstairs to get the girls out of the bath, dry and dress them and see them off to sleep with nursery rhymes and stories.

In bed, I reach for my book, *Middlemarch*, by George Eliot. Dorothea is a heroine I identify with. She dreams of a great future, of being of service to humanity. But she falls in love with Casaubon, an older man who is scholarly, pedantic, frigid and buried in his Great Work, to find the key to all mythologies. I used to dream too, before I left school and started to date boys. I dreamed of becoming a writer, of marrying a man who would see me deep beneath the surface and love me unconditionally, of living a life of art, romance and poetry. But I married a man like Casaubon, who is wrapped up in his work, to whom I am handmaid and helper and keeper of his household, who does not see my need for poetry and the magic of nature. Where is my Ladislaw, my artist, my poet?

Casaubon has died and Dorotha has been told of the condition in his will that, if she marries the handsome, passionate, idealistic young Will Ladislaw, she will not have a penny of the money left to her. I close the book and turn out the light, snuggling into the pillow. But my mind does not go to sleep. Robert's presence haunts me.

I got first-class honours in English literature and a teaching fellowship at Sydney University. I held that place for three years, trying to do a higher degree, but I was drifting. I'd give tutorials and the occasional lecture in English drama, the subject I was supposed to be doing my PhD in, I'd read Pinter and Beckett and the kitchen sink British dramatists, I'd hover on the edge of common room discussions about the latest literature theories, the new critics, and I'd wonder how I could write a thesis that would make a new contribution to scholarship. At home with Robert, I'd cook, clean, watch comedy shows with him, and type up his thesis, turning his turgid sentences into clear, readable prose. I didn't fit in his world, and I didn't fit in the world of academic English literature. I just wanted to read books and talk about poetry, novels, art and the meaning of life.

I knew I'd made a mistake marrying him. But I was hooked to his chariot, and his response to my restlessness was to give me an ultimatum.

We were sitting together on the rear deck of the ferry he'd hired to throw a farewell party for his best friend, who was returning to the West Indies. The ferry's horn blasted a small motorboat in its path as we passed under the Sydney Harbour Bridge. The night was sultry; the promised southerly buster hadn't arrived. Around us was the happy noise of people jiving to the Beatles. I'd been sitting on my own in a dark corner of the deck, away from the engine fumes, crying quietly. Robert had come to find me, to see why I wasn't joining in the dancing.

He lit a cigarette and leaned back on the canvas deck chair next to mine, exhaling slowly. 'Why are you crying?'

'I'm lonely.'

'I don't want you to be lonely. I know I've been at work a lot, getting the system up and running.' He blew out smoke rings, which drifted above us in the sultry salty air mixed with diesel fumes.

He's got no idea how I feel. For him, I'm a closed book, because he doesn't speak my language, or doesn't want to. We're poetry and science side by side on a bookshelf and we can't talk to each other. I might as well be one of his smoke rings.

'I've been thinking. We're going nowhere, you and me. You don't seem to be serious about the academic life,' he said, throwing his cigarette butt over the side of the boat.

He was right. I hadn't written any of my thesis yet, just an outline of the chapters, but I still hadn't found an argument to make about modern drama. As for teaching, I liked it, but sometimes I couldn't be bothered doing the preparation for it, and I'd ring up and say I was sick.

He said, 'We've been together over four years now. If we're going to stay together, I want to have children. Perhaps motherhood'll help you settle down.'

It was one of those moments in my life, like when he admitted to my mother that he planned to marry me, when I felt my life was mapped out for me and I just had to assent. I'd been crying for old dreams, for my loneliness. Perhaps that's all they would ever be, just dreams. Perhaps it was time I grew up. I'd resisted the idea of having children until that moment, because I was afraid of being locked into a lifetime with him. Yet, maybe he was right. Maybe having children would bring me to life, help me find myself. He is very forceful when he wants something. If I agreed to his wishes, I would not only make him happy, I might find a purpose in life. I took a deep breath.

As the ferry passed Bennelong Point, I said, 'Maybe you're right. Perhaps we should start a family.' I reached out and held his hand.

And so I had my first daughter and fell in love with her. He was right, I didn't feel lonely any more. I knew for the first time what it was to love another human being unconditionally. But my relationship with him, other than our shared parenthood, didn't change. He didn't open up to me and I didn't open up to him. He focused on his work and on Sophia when he was at home, and I focused on mothering Sophia and soothing her through her colic, which she suffered from night and day. I sang myself back into babyhood, into being nurtured and held, into being safe and loved and wanted.

I've never been able to talk to Robert about things I'm interested in. Just this morning, as we sat in bed sipping cups of tea made by our bedside teamaking machine, a wedding present he had chosen, he started on his pet theme.

'In twenty years' time, computers'll do most of the work. People'll have to learn to use their leisure more creatively.' He poured himself some more tea.

'You mean like writing poetry and painting?'

'No way. Most people don't have the type of brain that can appreciate works of art and literature. Let alone create them! The place for things like that will be in libraries, museums, art galleries. No, most people'll want to be entertained, so TV and other forms of electronic media'll be the rage. As for poetry, computers'll be so smart they'll do it better than a person could.' He recited this as if he was on stage, gesturing with his left hand, conjuring up his vision of Utopia.

'Oh, Robert, come on,' I said, as I put my dressing gown on. 'No computer in a million years could write a play like *Hamlet*, or a novel like *Anna Karenina*!'

'Why not?' He leaned back on the pillow and watched me as I searched for my slippers under the bed.

'Because computers don't have a heart, a soul, or a flesh-and-blood brain.'

'Well, you're right there. But there's a whole new science called artificial intelligence. Who knows what we'll be able to achieve with that?'

'Not works of art,' I said, walking out the bedroom door.

*

It's another golden Sunday. Robert will be busy putting the last touches to his paper in his hotel room overlooking Lake Windermere.

'Mummy!' Caitlin runs in from the playroom, eyes sparkling, flossed red curls catching the rays of sunlight slanting across the room. 'Can we go to Nell's and spend our sixpences?'

With Penelope in the stroller, we trail over to Nell's across the road. Nell's shop is a relic of the days when the village was centred round rural life, before it became a dormitory town for London, which is an hour away by train. Nell greets us in her thick Berkshire accent, with nods and smiles for the girls. She had polio as a child and is very lame. Mostly she sits behind her little counter, and when a customer wants something, she directs them to the cluttered shelves around the room. If you want a less sought-after item, like hairpins, light bulbs, safety pins, cotton thread, matches, shoe polish, she indicates the exact position where it can be found in the store room behind. To find it, you have to brave spiderwebs, the smell of mice, and the risk of surprising one at work. The food she keeps in the front room is of varying ages. The fresh stock is stacked in front of cakes growing mould, potatoes and onions sprouting green shoots, tins rusting and thick with dust and cobwebs. The lollies are a safe purchase. Nell does a brisk trade in them, and a few items like daily milk and bread. The children love her, and she is infinitely patient with their lengthy transactions.

Caitlin has chosen her lollies, a Wagon Wheel and a Milko. Penelope wants an ice cream, so I help her pick one from the freezer cabinet. Sophia asks for a Kit Kat.

We set off back to the farmhouse. The shadows lengthen and the evening chill rises. Caitlin, who has finished her lollies already, runs over to gather some conkers from under the horse chestnut trees and stuffs them in her pinafore pockets.

'Me! Conker!' Penelope cries.

Sophia gathers a few and plonks them in Penelope's lap.

If Robert were here, he wouldn't have joined in this little excursion. He'd be working on the new software he's developing for the lab's remote network, so officers can enter their data from home. Like him, I imagine, most of them work after hours and at weekends. I once asked him if he wanted more time at home to spend with his family.

'Oh, maybe when I get this system up and working the way I want it to. For now, it's the most important thing I have to do. It's what I came here for, and I have to show I can do it. This is the way that future offices will run. We won't need to go to work, even for meetings. We can have meetings online. We'll be able to see each other and talk as if we're in the same room.'

Well, at least for now, the girls and I have our home to ourselves, and I've turned the console off for the day. This morning, I made scones, and we'll have them with jam and cream for afternoon tea.

'Come on, girls. I've got a treat for you.'

*

A week later, Robert is back. He walks in and takes off his sheepskin coat and gloves and hat. The energy in the house changes; there's a tightness in the air, and I take some deep breaths to ease the tension in my chest. I close my book and stand up. I'd reached the part where Dorothea has realised that she loves Ladislaw and is determined to free herself from the yoke Casaubon had placed on her. But that's a novel, and my husband is still alive.

He drops his suitcase and holds his arms out, pulling me in to his side, kissing my mouth. 'I've missed you!'

'How was the conference?' I say, stepping away to call the children in from the garden. He'll want to have sex tonight. When he kisses me on the mouth, I know he's thinking about it.

'Excellent! My paper was well received, and I met up again with a professor from New York who's interested in getting me over there soon to set up a similar system for their department.'

I guess that means he'll be away again soon, I hope for longer this time.

While he greets the children with hugs and kisses and little gifts, a tea set for the Wendy house and a wooden cat puzzle for Penelope, I go to the kitchen and put the kettle on. Outside, the sky is looming low and there's a hush in the air. The terracotta tiles on the gable roof over the kitchen are creaking; I've noticed they do this when snow is coming. Perhaps they contract against the cold.

A knock at the door startles me. We hardly ever have uninvited visitors. Robert's upstairs unpacking, Penelope's on the floor with the puzzle, and the older girls are in the playroom with their new toys. I go to the door.

A tall, slim man with long legs and a shock of curly dark brown hair is standing on the step, hands in the pockets of his hand-knitted cardigan. He greets me with a wide smile. He wears dark-rimmed glasses like Buddy Holly. I take a step back, startled. For a moment, I am a teenager again in bobby socks and flared skirt, caught up in the dream of young love, first love.

'Hello, I'm Derek, from across the road at the end house.' He reaches out his hand, grasping mine. His fingers are warm. 'You've been our neighbours for over a year now – I've seen you coming and going. I thought it's about time I get to know you.'

I introduce Caitlin and Sophia, who have run out to see who it is. Sophia hangs back, peeping at the visitor through her long fringe, her mouth curled into a shy smile, her fingers touching my skirt. Caitlin gazes up at Derek's face so far above her and gives one of her radiant grins. They soon lose interest and go back to their game of shopping and keeping house. Penelope pulls herself up by gripping my skirt, and I take her in my arms.

Derek follows me to the kitchen and watches while I put the teapot and biscuits on the tea trolley. He says, 'This is the first time I've been in Walnut Tree Farmhouse since the cockneys started to renovate it. I'm an industrial designer, so I'm curious to see what they've done. It was pretty run-down when they came here.'

In the living room, as I pour Derek's tea, Robert walks in. He scans the visitor's tall frame and nods. His face is unsmiling, he seems tense. They briefly shake hands.

After tea, Robert takes Derek on a tour of the house, and I hear their voices rising and falling in dissent. Tea things cleared away, I bring out the sherry glasses and decanter. The men return to the living room, where they continue to spar words while I sit on the floor with Penelope, playing pat-a-cake.

While Derek talks, I see, out of the corner of my eye, that he is gazing at me, has moved closer to me. Robert stands back, watching us both. I drop my eyes and bury my face in Penelope's curls. The two are opposite to each other physically as well as in their ideas – Derek tall and lean, Robert short and decidedly paunchy. Only his legs are as thin as when I met him. Derek's voice attracts me…he has a public school accent, but there's a Berkshire lilt underneath. His face is lively, his eyes soft, like melted chocolate. I don't listen to what they're saying, just the rise and fall of his voice, in counterpoint to Robert, whose sentences have a rising inflection like a question wanting an answer, except when he's delivering information.

After Derek leaves, Robert pours himself another sherry and sits down with Penelope on his lap while I pick up toys with Sophia and Caitlin.

He pulls Derek's card out of his pocket. 'Hmph. Derek Knightley. Industrial and interior designer. I reckon he's a bit of a know-all. Thinks he knows everything about old houses, though I notice he lives in a modern one himself. He couldn't take his eyes off you.'

When we go to bed, he reaches for me. 'Come here.' He pulls my nightie off and slides on top of me. Soon he is thrusting, gasping and groaning. His idea of preliminaries is a few kisses and groping my breasts and pubis.

I hold him and wait for him to finish. I respond to his thrusts, so that he will climax sooner. Spent, he murmurs goodnight and turns over to sleep.

As I drift off to sleep, I think of long legs, liquid brown eyes, and a lilting voice.

Two

Lately, I've felt lost, drifting, aware there are so many things I could be doing in the house and garden, yet unable to find the energy or the will to throw myself into anything. When I do start a task, like clearing out the summer clothes the girls have grown out of, I feel anxious and tense because of all the other things I could or should be doing and am not – writing to Mum, finishing Sophia's bunny, making Christmas puddings, sending Christmas cards. Sometimes, the emptiness inside presses on my chest as though it will break through and destroy the life that seems to have been chosen for me.

Robert was my mother's choice for a husband. I've often thought they should have been man and wife, were it not for the generation gap. He has great respect for her, her intellect, her rationality, her determination. She admires his ambition and drive, and his powerful intelligence. She couldn't have him herself, so I was her stand-in. She called him late one night when I was in bed with him at his flat and insisted he bring me home. When we got there, she questioned him about his intentions and declared we should get married before the end of the year. We've been together twelve years now, and he has been a good provider and a good father when he is home. But I am an actor in his story, where I keep his domestic world together. Within that, there is another story with my daughters at the centre of it and he is peripheral. I lie awake at night and dream of a different life, where they are still with me and he is gone. Where I don't feel I am playing a part.

I feel tense all the time, and have trouble sleeping. I start having lessons in the Alexander technique, a way of retraining the body to shed lifelong, unconscious patterns of movement and posture, to bring the body under conscious control. I am fascinated by the rituals of sitting, standing and lying that my elderly teacher patiently puts me through, but I feel little change in my daily life. The tension is locked deep inside me like a tightly coiled spring, a hidden machine I have no control over and do not know how to shift.

On a damp and misty November day, when the girls are at school, I decide to shake off my depression by taking Penelope to the village to buy bread and milk. As I push the stroller out of the muddy driveway into the road, Derek steps out of the mist.

'Hello! What have you done to yourself?' He is staring at my bruised face.

'I had some moles cut out a few days ago. I'm to have the stitches out tomorrow.'

'For a minute, I thought you'd been bashed up! Can I walk with you?'

Mist rolls away from the road as late morning sunlight warms the air. He tells me about his work. He is trying to build a business designing and constructing furniture. To make ends meet, he produces knick-knacks like coin savers and wine racks.

'Marion helps me with it. She's a potter, does some fine stuff, but it doesn't sell well – it's too abstract for most people.'

He tells me he's been married eight years and they've got three kids. 'They've kept us poor and busy! Robert seems successful. He must work pretty hard.'

'Seven days a week. He's away a lot, too.'

'D'you get lonely, looking after three kids on your own?'

'It's hard... I don't have any family here.'

He reaches out and grasps my hand, his long, calloused fingers around my small, cold ones. I leave my hand there for a moment, then grasp the back of the stroller. We come to a stop at the stream. Geese waddle over, looking for bread. Penelope begins to cry.

'I'd better go and do my shopping. Thanks for walking with me.'

Sometimes when I'm upstairs in the morning and the girls are getting ready for school, I walk into the spare room, which has a big window overlooking the front garden. I can see Derek's house from here, and I watch for him to drive past, taking his kids to school. He always turns his head and looks for me. I feel like the Lady of Shallott, stepping forward to gaze at the bold knight passing by. I know that as I do so, I endanger this world that has been created for me and my children.

Christmas comes and goes, and icy winds keep us indoors. Robert leaves for work early in the mornings and comes home late every night, perfecting the system he's going to show off to a New York group of computer scientists. I find myself wishing for him to go and not come back.

After a flurry of packing and last-minute checking of data on the console, he's standing at the living room window, waiting for a taxi to come and take him to the airport. He seems more wound up than usual.

'I'll ring you once a week on Sunday evening. Look after yourself and the girls and stay warm. I've left enough money in the account for a month's housekeeping.'

He kisses me on the cheek and turns to the girls, who are watching a cartoon. They let him kiss and hug them and turn back to the TV screen. He's been away so much lately, they barely notice he's gone.

*

New Year's Eve is coming, and I expect to see it in alone. But I bump into Derek in the village, and he invites me to spend the evening with him and Marion.

Soft snowflakes drift down as I walk across to the end house. The girls are tucked up warm in bed; the babysitter is settled in with her knitting, watching soapies on TV. Derek greets me at the door, taking my coat, pressing my mittened hand in his large, warm one. Marion steps out into the hallway and greets me. She is short, like me, and plain, with collar-length hair worn in a bob. She has a masculine face, with a strong jaw and hooked nose.

After a glass or two of wine, I relax and begin to enjoy the company. I feel they are both wooing me. Marion talks freely about her work as a potter and life with Derek when they were both students at tech. He is quieter, but I feel his attention fixed on me, though he is careful not to gaze at me too much.

They talk about their attractions to other people while they were in college.

'We weren't a couple at first,' Derek says, stretching his legs.

'No,' Marion says, 'you were in love with Meredith of the bouncy bum and glossy brown curls, and I was in love with her too.'

'So how did you get together?' I ask, sipping mulled wine, taking a slice of brie and a water biscuit from the platter in front of the fire.

She looks at me, lets her eyes linger on my face and throat, and smiles. 'I got pregnant. Derek and I talked about it, and decided it was most likely his, so we agreed to be faithful to each other and have the baby.'

Derek's eyes are on the fire.

'How did you feel, Derek?' I say.

'Oh, Marion and I had a lot of fun together and shared ideas about art and design, and it seemed like something we could do together. We still got attracted to other people, but Marion kept me in tow. Somehow it lasted until we got married.'

I wonder what he means by that. Don't they desire each other any more? Is he tired of the marriage? Does he feel trapped, like me?

I think of my secret life, the fantasies I have about a lover who would see me for who I am (if only I knew myself!) and would share soul dreams with me. It doesn't sound like these two have that kind of a relationship. Sounds more pragmatic. I could talk about my marriage, my regret for not having given myself more time to be free like they were at college. But I don't feel safe enough to be honest about it. She keeps her eyes fixed on me, and I wonder if she desires me, or if she is jealous of Derek's attention.

This is not the time for true confessions. I hardly know them.

Derek puts on a record – José Feliciano's 'Light My Fire'. I find the blind singer's voice insubstantial, but I enjoy the Latin rhythm of his guitar and feel there is a message for me in the words. I am warm and relaxed. The knot in my stomach has gone, the open fire radiates warmth, and Robert is far away.

We've drained the last drops of wine, played José for the third time. I stretch, yawn, murmur I must go home.

Derek stands up and kisses Marion on the cheek. 'I'll just see Anna home, love.'

We drift home under a dark sky, our feet falling on powdery snow. His hand rests under my elbow, his curly head towers above mine as we talk about inconsequential things. We reach the back of the farmhouse. As I lift my keys towards the door, I am clasped by two long arms and kissed, passionately, with warm open mouth. After a moment, I pull away, fumble with the key, say goodbye, don't look up at him.

This is the first time I've been kissed by another man since I married Robert. Perhaps I am just one in a chain, and they tolerate each other's digressions. I want not to feel guilty, to yield to his desire. But I also want to be the only one.

I ask Marion to coffee one morning, and while our kids play together, I come clean. 'Marion…I think you should know…I think Derek's attracted to me. He kissed me when he walked me home. I don't know what to do about it. You know how we talked on New Year's Eve about attractions you and he had to other people when you were at college together?'

'Ye-es?' she says cautiously, looking at me under frowning brows.

'Has he said anything to you about me?'

'Hmmph! He's all talk and no action. He likes to make eyes at women from time to time, but if anyone took him seriously, he'd run a mile!'

Though this isn't the answer my conscience wants, the dreamer in me is relieved. Marion's overconfident attitude hardens me towards her. I can't bring myself to say I am attracted to him. I feel less guilty because she doesn't know her own husband. Just as mine doesn't know me. I begin to justify the idea of having an affair with him, although I am still confused, unsure of what I want.

I try to hold on to my everyday self and the outline of my days with tasks like shopping and meeting Caitlin and Sophia on their way home from school with their friend Jane.

One wet January day, when I am walking with Penelope to meet the girls, Derek's old station wagon pulls up beside me and he steps out.

'Anna! I've been hoping to see you. I want to talk to you.'

My heart turns over; this feels like a moment of choice. He is a stranger to me, but we have touched each other, and the vibration has made my world wobble.

'I can't keep hoping to bump into you on the road. I can't sleep. I can't think straight.'

The rain, which has been soft and fine, begins blowing in my face, running in rivulets down my glasses. My nose closes against the cold air, and I turn to face the pushchair away from the direction of the rain. Derek steps up beside me so that his body shields me from the rain's force.

I stand poised in this wintry world, remembering times when I've felt a thrill of desire, and times when I've felt betrayed. I think of how I felt on my wedding day, how I felt when we'd been married six months and I realised I had made a mistake. I think of our daughters and of the life we lead, a beautiful life in many ways, and yet, outside the core of my love for my children, my heart feels empty. I think of how Robert told me about the affair he'd had when I was pregnant with Penelope; how betrayed I felt.

'Sorry…it's hard to think in this weather! I'm on my way to meet the girls. They'll be wondering where I am.'

'Let me give you a lift.' He guides me over to the car and puts the stroller in the back while I climb into the front seat with Penelope.

We drive towards the school, and I see Sophia, Caitlin, and Jane, huddling together, heads bent against the rain, running towards us. Derek jumps out and helps them into the back seat.

'Mu-um?'

'Yes, Sophia?'

'Can Jane come and play for a while?'

I know Jane's parents won't worry about where she is as long as she is home by dark. The humid air in the car, with the heater on, is stuffy and smelly. I turn my head to see three faces looking hopefully at me.

'Yes, of course.'

Sophia and Caitlin bounce up and down and exchange smiles with Jane.

I feel safe with him in this old metal and steel cage rattling down the bumpy road, splashing through little lakes of water, rain hammering on the roof and washing down the windows. When we turn into the Walnut Tree driveway, I turn my head towards the house, this dream of England I share with Robert and the girls. I've briefly entered a movie, a romance, and now I have to step out of it, back into normal life. My girls need me, they are the centre of my life, and this is an illusion, sitting here beside him as if we are a family.

We get out of the car and Derek hands me the stroller. His hair is dishevelled, rain drips down his face.

'Thanks for the lift. You saved us from drowning!'

His eyes behind his wet spectacles plead with me. 'Please! Say when you'll meet me! Do you ever go to London?' He takes his glasses off and wipes them with a crumpled hanky.

I have to go to London to be briefed for marking English O level papers. So I agree to meet him.

He reminds me of what I lost so long ago when my father left – instinctual, earthy love, the feeling of being cherished, even adored – but he is not mine.

*

While in the city, I visit the famous Leonard's of London. The hairdresser styles my hair in a long feather cut, shoulder-length, but layered so that the natural wave breaks up the fall. Washed and dried, it is shining golden brown, and I feel beautiful.

I walk to Regent Park to meet Derek, and we spend our two stolen hours together, lying under a spell, his warm greatcoat spread over us, holding each other, talking a little. The weather is kind, it does not rain, and the hum of traffic is muted by the soft sound of little waves on the banks of the lake, stirred up by a small wind and the calls of water birds.

In the train on the way home, I stare out at the world through watered glass. Fields, hedges and sky are spread out in muted colours, soft browns, deep greens and greys, veiled by misty rain. The wintry monotony of earth and sky through the rain-blurred window reminds me paradoxically of the dry Hay Plains, and the many times I sat in the train, coming back from boarding school or visits to the coast, glad to see again the familiar bare, stark landscape.

The train is pulling into my station. I shake myself and turn my mind to home and the children. He has come into my life all of a sudden and has made it seem empty without him. Though our worlds are side by side, touching each other, I doubt we can be other than visitors in each other's lives. And I dread the uproar we might cause.

Three

Robert is back from New York. While dinner is cooking, he plays with the children and I stand in the kitchen, shelling peas, wondering what Derek is doing. I think there will be snow tonight; the evening sky is low, thick grey cloud cover hanging over the fields. The air is a little warmer, and there was a moist feel on my face and hands when I went out to shut the chooks in.

Derek is probably still at his workshop, the old mill outside the village, working on a big order. I haven't seen him again since our tryst in London. I said I wanted to wait till Robert came home, and I need to think some more about us. I felt it would be wrong to become Derek's lover while Robert was away. I even wondered if I should talk to Robert about it first, let him know how I feel, see whether we can make a new start to our marriage. Lately, the children are all that's been holding us together, that and our friends, this house, our social life. And he's been away so much.

'Anna! he calls. 'Come and join us. I've got some surprises.'

I turn the gas low under the stew and join him and the children in the living room. He opens a large, shiny leather briefcase and pulls out parcels.

'Oh, I like your briefcase. Did you get it in New York?'

'Yeah…it was a going-away gift.'

'From the guys you were working with?'

'Sort of.' He hands me a paper bag.

'Bloomingdale's! Wow.' I pull out a black garment. A jumpsuit, stretchy and close-fitting. I've never worn one like this. I've fallen in love with English woollen fabrics and hand-knits.

'Do you like it?' Robert says, reaching for the sherry decanter and pouring us a generous glass each.

'Oh, I'm not sure. I haven't worn anything like that before. I'll try it on after. Did you choose it yourself?' He never normally buys me clothes.

'Err...no, I got a friend to choose it. She's about your height and shape. It looked good on her.' His eyes are fixed on his sherry glass, and there's a hint of a smile around his mouth.

He pulls out some bags and gives the girls one each and one to share. The shared one has candies – 'For after dinner, girls!' There's a Barbie doll each for Caitlin and Sophia, and a cute Baby Bear pair of onesies for Penelope. 'Hugs for Daddy!'

They cluster round him. Sophia and Caitlin clutch their dolls and run off to the playroom. Penelope insists I dress her in the onesie, and snuggles happily on Robert's knee while we talk.

I feel there's more to the briefcase and the jumpsuit. Before, when we've been apart, he's had affairs, I know, though he only told me about one of them, the one with Marie.

After the girls are in bed, Robert pours us each a cognac and tells me to go upstairs and put the jumpsuit on. I feel strange, wriggling into it and pulling the zipper up. I've lost the extra weight I put on when I was pregnant, so it fits OK. I stand under the oak beams, looking into the mirror. Is that me? I look taller and slimmer, a bit like a hooker. I slip on my black shoes – low heels, I can't wear stillettos, and go downstairs.

'Wow!' says Robert, his eyes running up and down my body. 'You're slimmer than I thought!'

'Slimmer than the woman who modelled it for you?'

'Oh...she's skinnier than you. But then, she hasn't had children.' He fidgets with his brandy balloon and puts it down on the bar, lights himself a cigar. He settles back on the sofa and pats the seat beside him.

'So, did you have an affair with her?' I wouldn't normally be so blunt, but past experience and thoughts of Derek prompt me to go straight to the point. I actually want to hear that he's fallen in love again. This could be my get out of jail card.

He takes a long swig of cognac and a couple of puffs on his cigar.

'Well, yes. We had a lot in common. She's working on computer systems too. She's a few years younger…'

'Younger than me?'

'Yes, she's only twenty-five. She's come out of a bad relationship, and we just…we clicked.'

'Are you going to see her again?'

'No. I told her I won't do anything to break up my family. She's still young, she can find someone who'll make her happy. It was hard. She couldn't stop crying when we said goodbye. I cried too.'

I feel cold and detached. I stay home and keep the family together, while he builds his career, goes to conferences at home and abroad, works long hours, and comes home in between. The children don't notice when he is away, it is so routine. He is their fun Daddy, who reappears from time to time, smothering them with gifts and affection, then disappears again. This time he went away, I hoped that the plane would crash, or he'd have an accident or sudden fatal illness. But he always comes back. Perhaps he feels empty, that he's not loved by me in the way he wants to be. But he does nothing to connect with me, other than going through the motions when he's around. He doesn't help with any of the housework or cooking. He will dress the girls sometimes and put them to sleep with tales and little songs and do occasional DIY tasks. He built wall-to-wall cupboards in the girls' room when he had some holidays. It was a huge job, and he did it really well. Anything he undertakes, he finishes. It's the little things I miss, conversations, affectionate gestures, laughs, outings together, help with daily chores when he's home; I can't expect deep, meaningful discussions with him, but at least I'd like companionship.

I empty my glass and take it to the kitchen.

'Well, Robert, I've nothing to say. I've heard this story before,' I say as I walk towards the hall. If I go to bed now, I should be asleep when he comes up.

He gives me one of his frowning gazes and pours himself another cognac.

I'm drifting off to sleep when he climbs in beside me. He reaches for me.

I roll away and get out of bed. 'Goodnight, Robert. I'm going to sleep in the spare room from now on.'

I lie in bed in the big, cold room, unrestored, lino on the floor, no beamed ceiling here, just a bed and a table and some old curtains across the window that looks across to the Endhouse on the other side of the road. I wonder what Derek is doing now, if he's making love with Marion. I wonder how they make love.

My mind is made up. I'll watch out for Derek tomorrow and let him know.

Four

I waved to Derek as he drove past this morning. We'd agreed that I would wave with both hands if I was free to meet him. I leave Penelope with the housekeeper and walk the girls up to school. He's there in his wagon, waiting for me.

'Where are we going?' I snuggle up close to him on the bench seat of the car and put my mittened hand on his knee. It's a day of sleet and icy winds, after the snowfall last night.

'I thought just out of town a bit to a quiet field I know where we can park under some old oak trees.' He's wearing ugg boots, cords, a thick cabled wool jumper, and a ribbed cap pulled over his ears. His curls escape from under it, his lips are soft and moist.

'Robert came back yesterday.'

'Yes, I saw him drive out in the bus this morning. How was it between you?'

'Oh, usual story. He brought presents back and told me about an affair he had in New York.'

'What a homecoming gift! How did you feel?'

'Very little. It's happened before.'

Derek turns into a field a couple of miles out of town and parks the wagon under a huge old oak tree bordering a little stream. 'It'll be sheltered from the wind here.'

He shuffles across from behind the steering wheel and we wrap ourselves around each other. I pull off my boots and slide my left leg over his. He takes off his cap and shakes his curls free, warm brown silk. We kiss and I run my fingers through his stubbly beard.

'Sweetheart, will you make love with me?' He runs his hand up my thigh, and I quiver. He looks at me while his fingers stroke me, his eyes deep and soft.

'I…I want to, but I'm afraid.'

'What are you afraid of?'

'I can't say… Once we make love, we can't go back to how we were.'

'How we were is gone already. How I was is gone. I met you, and nothing was the same any more. Please?'

He kisses me again and my fear melts away.

The lovemaking is brief and awkward, with me straddled across his lap, my tights down around my ankles. He comes quickly, and we stay wrapped together while he strokes me.

'I'm sorry,' he murmurs. 'I'm not usually like this…it's just…'

'No matter,' I say. 'There's not much scope on the front seat of the car. It's lovely just to be so close to you.' I'm not really disappointed, as I didn't know what to expect. I would have been quite content just to hold and kiss each other and talk.

'It's important to give a woman pleasure,' he says. 'I work hard to give Marion pleasure. Our sex is more intense now, because it's you I'm holding and caressing when I'm with her.'

I can't answer this. What does it mean, that he makes love to his wife while thinking of me? I can't do that. I can't separate the act of sexual intercourse from love any more. Is this a difference between men and women? That they need sex more than they need love?

But I hope that we can find a safe place to be together, somehow, between two worlds, his marriage and my marriage. Where I can learn what it is to know someone deeply and to love and be loved.

Our next meeting is at the old mill where he has his workshop. I escape from home, leaving the children in Robert's care one wet Sunday afternoon, on the pretext of going to see my housekeeper, who is ill with bronchitis. I climb the spiral staircase to the whine of a saw and smells of resin and something acrid…glue? The light is dim, and Derek's tall shape is etched against the cobwebbed window. He steps forward and wraps his arms round me. His curls have wood shavings in them. Soon we are wrapped together in the dust of old wooden floorboards. The fragrant smells of cedar and pine mix with musky smell of his body.

His hands are warm and the hairs on his arms are filmed with sawdust. Our lovemaking, again, is brief. He lies with his arms wrapped around me, his face buried in my breasts.

'I love you so much, I know I can't keep you with me, so I just…I can't hold back.'

'Darling, someday, perhaps, we'll have longer together.'

The passion and secrecy of our meeting is more exciting than the act itself. He feels too much, I don't feel much physically. I think it's fear of losing him that numbs me.

Nearing home, I am driving our VW bus along a narrow winding road bordered by snow-covered hedges. The road is slippery and as I negotiate a curve, the back wheels of the bus slide out and I nearly lose control. Shaken, I manage to stop, and sit for a few minutes reviewing my life. What will happen to the children if I don't come home? How will Robert look after them? How will Derek feel? He will probably hang on to a few romantic memories and get on with his life with Marion.

Oh God, I can't keep doing this. I'll have to tell Robert. I can't keep up this double life, half-life.

We meet again in his car, this time at night in a field off the road to Oxford. Robert has been away on a two-day work thing, due back tomorrow. My housekeeper's teenage daughter is babysitting.

'I waited under the horse chestnut trees outside your front garden to make sure you got home safely last time,' he says, running his fingers through my hair.

'Oh, you're sweet. I didn't see you as I drove in. My shadow lover!'

We don't attempt to make love this time, just sit entwined in each other's arms, kissing, sometimes just resting our cheeks together. All we need is time, freedom, and the right to be together to make our dreams come true. His words of love spin a web around me more powerful than any physical expression. He doesn't talk about making love to Marion any more, and I think that if we have time together, those doubts and insecurities will fall away. His eagerness, his apologies, endear him to me far more than polished technique and subtle arts could do.

'Derek, I can't go on like this. I'll have to tell Robert. I don't really care any more about how he reacts.'

'Sweetheart, I know. I've been thinking that too. Marion and I are in a rut. We work hard, we try to pay the bills, to bring up our kids well, but whatever there was between us when we got together has vanished. We sparkled at first, but once we got married, the stardust fell away.'

'Do you think she'll be upset?'

'To tell the truth, I don't know if she's ever loved me. She's had a few crushes on other men, and one or two on women. I don't know if she's had sex with them or not. She actually fancies you, you know!'

'Oh, I wondered about that, that New Year's evening. But then I thought maybe she just kept her eyes on me because she was jealous.'

'Anyway, we're going nowhere as we are. I'll talk to her tomorrow.'

'Do you think we can live together? If she agrees to separate?'

'She's a strange one. I don't know what's going on in her head a lot of the time. But she's worked very hard and supported me with my business, and she might be glad to be free of that and focus on her pottery. What about Robert?'

'Well, he adores his kids. As for me, I'm a token wife and someone to have sex with. I don't think he loves me, if he ever did. How could he, and fall in love with two other women?'

'Maybe we could find an old farmhouse to live in round here, and you could have your kids with you, they could still see him, and my kids could visit. Do you like old houses?'

'I like them better than modern houses. I don't need much. As long as we can have an open fire, and some fields around us!'

We hug and kiss again and I try not to think about the next step.

'Well, love, I'd better take you home.'

The night is wild with bitter wind.

*

When Robert comes home next day, we don't say much. He seems preoccupied and more distant than usual. After the girls are in bed asleep, I ask him to turn off the TV and sit with me for a few minutes. My throat is dry, my heart is racing. I take some deep breaths.

'Robert, I must tell you, Derek and I have fallen in love. I don't want to keep deceiving you.'

He lights a cigarette and stares out the window. 'Hmm. I thought there was something going on. How many times have you been together?

'Oh, not many. We saw each other last night and agreed to come clean.'

'You must be dreaming. He's struggling to make a living, he's got a wife and three kids, they're probably in debt up to their ears. He's got nothing to offer you.' He turns and looks at me. His mouth is tight, his eyes are frosty blue. 'What is it you want?'

'I want to be with someone I love, someone I can talk to, someone I can be fully myself with.'

'So, he's a better lover than me?'

'I didn't say that. But…I don't love you. I don't want to have sex with you any more.'

'You've already made that clear. I told you I'll do nothing to break up the family.' He stubs out his cigarette in the glass ashtray and stands up.

'Robert, if you think having a family is about going to work all the time, being away, having affairs when you want to, and coming home to your wife and kids, it's not my idea of a marriage.'

'You don't have a clue what my life is like. Everything I've worked for has been for you and the girls.' His voice is shaking.

'Well, you think you're a good husband and father. I'm not going to argue with you. Let's talk about it some more tomorrow.'

He goes to the bar to pour a drink, and I go up to the spare room. In bed, I wonder if Derek has spoken to Marion yet.

*

Two days later, Marion and Derek come over together. When the children are in the playroom, we sit around the dining table. Derek stares at the table, his face a mask. Marion avoids my eyes and looks at Robert.

'Derek's told me all about his meetings with Anna. We've talked it through and decided that we don't want to separate and break up our family. We love each other and intend to stay together.'

I don't hear the rest of the conversation. Derek won't meet my eyes. Robert and Marion do all the talking.

After they've gone, Robert turns to me. 'Well, so much for your lover. He didn't have a word to say for himself, for once!'

'I don't want to talk about it, Robert. I've got papers to mark. I'm going upstairs.'

Some years, I mark O level English for the London Board of Examiners. The trip to London when I met Derek was for a briefing on marking standards. The papers came last week, and I've been struggling to get them done on time. It was hard to focus on them before, because I was thinking of Derek. Now, I just feel numb. I stare at the handwritten scrawl and try to remember what the exam question was.

I imagine Robert's working at the console and the girls are playing Barbie dolls or mothers and fathers with Penelope. After a while, I hear the television…cartoons – an hour earlier than I would turn them on. I force myself to do another hour of marking. Five o'clock comes, and I go down to the kitchen to heat up our tea, leftover shepherd's pie. I can't eat much, so I leave Robert and the girls at the table and serve some custard and sponge pudding.

'I have to do some more marking,' I say, putting the pudding in front of them. 'Robert, can you give them a bath and put them to bed? I'll come and say goodnight when they're ready.'

He looks up, nods, and helps Penelope with the last of her peas and pie.

I'm walking in a winter world, waiting for the ice to break under my feet.

*

It is seven o'clock on a bleak, dark, February morning of hoar frost and sub-zero temperature. I stand outside the end house. My nose, swollen and red from crying all night, goes into spasms, sharp needling pain shooting up and closing my nostrils. I can't get my breath. I clasp my mittened hands over my nose to warm it up. My fingers are numb. I shake my head and take a breath. Stepping up to the door, I thrust a bulky brown envelope through the mail slot in the door. It slides through and falls on the wooden floor inside with a clatter. There is no sound in the house, but I imagine Derek waking and creeping downstairs to pick up the envelope, knowing who it is from. In it are his grandmother's Victorian amethyst beads, which he gave me as a keepsake last time we met. Amethyst is my birthstone. They are beautiful, large and smooth with a deep rich glow. I hid them in a drawer in the spare room. I've been sleeping with them under a pillow. I'll never wear them now.

I turn, crunching my way back along the path, up the frost-hard laneway to the house across the road, to my sleeping children and husband.

I see nothing of Derek for at least a month, except for the sight of his station wagon roaring past in the morning. He doesn't turn his head to look for me any more. I spend my days trying to meet the deadline for marking O level papers. I pay the housekeeper to look after the children.

I feel betrayed, abandoned, unable to understand how he can allow Marion to dictate to him; I believe he was a passive partner in the agreement. He hasn't even had the courage to speak for himself, to tell me directly why he chooses to drop me.

I remember what it felt like to be loved, to be held in my father's warm arms in a circle of mutual trust and delight. But he left when I was seven, walked away from our home on the riverbank, trudging across the paddocks, carrying a suitcase. He left a note for me, in an envelope with the mouth organ he used to play in the evenings. We didn't say goodbye properly. I knew he was going and I wanted to go with him. But he told me I had to stay with my mother and look after her. 'I don't know where I'll be living,' he said, 'and I won't have a house of my own for a while.'

So I ran down to the bend and sat in my favourite tree until the sun was setting. When I came back to the house, his bedroom was empty, the bed stripped, his clothes gone except for an old pair of work trousers and a tattered shirt. They smelt of his sweat and tobacco.

For days after he left, when my work was done, I wandered up and down the driveway, straining to see if a car was approaching the road into our place, playing mournful laments with no beginning and no ending on the mouth organ. I hoped he would return.

When things failed with Derek, I told myself that like my father, he never really loved me – he only cared about himself. And so he can drop me, just like that, just like my father, and not look back. And not even talk to me or explain or help me to understand. All the wild grief and despair I felt as a child comes back, and I feel more trapped than ever in my marriage.

Five

Robert begins wooing me, realising he is in danger of losing the world he has built. 'Anna, if we're going to stay together, I...I need to talk to you.' He hands me a cup of tea and sits on the bed in the spare room

I'm trying to get the last batch of marking finished. I hold my breath for a moment, then turn to him. 'Robert, can't it wait? I have to finish these by the weekend.'

'No, I'm going to Germany soon for a conference.'

'Oh, when?'

'Err, next week.' He slicks his hair across his brow. 'Look...I realise I've not been a good husband. I work too hard, I'm away a lot, I...I've neglected you.'

I say nothing.

'W-will you give me another chance?'

'Robert, I don't want to talk about it. Please leave me alone.'

He takes a mouthful of tea and clears his throat. 'You...you don't have orgasms, do you?'

'No, I don't.'

'Well, I saw the doctor yesterday and told him we're having difficulties. He lent me this book. He said that frigidity in women is a common problem, and, um, he said I should buy you a vibrator.' He holds the book out to me.

Everything You Always Wanted to Know about Sex but Were Afraid to Ask, by David Reuben. I look at it but don't take it from him. 'It's not about technique. Look, I've got work to do. Maybe we can talk about this when you come back from Germany.'

He tosses the book on the bed and walks out of the room.

Next day, I find a massage machine on my bed. It's meant for body massage, but I suppose he didn't want to go to a sex shop to get one. I put it in the cupboard under some clothes. Maybe I am frigid, but if I am, he hasn't got the key to unlock my desire, and I wouldn't care if I never had sex again. We haven't had sex since before he went to New York.

I heat up a frozen meal for him and the children and retreat to my room again. When they're in bed after their bath, I go in and cuddle them and tell them a story. When Robert comes in, I say goodnight to them.

'I'm on the last lap of marking,' I say to Robert, 'so I'd better go and finish. Please put Penelope to bed.' I give her a last hug and kiss and hand her to him. 'Night, darlings, sleep well.'

I sit up till nearly midnight marking the last few papers and writing an examiner's report. Sometime in the pre-dawn hours, I wake from fitful sleep to find him kneeling beside my bed. He's crying.

'Please, let me make love to you. I can't bear it any more. Please f-forgive me for having been so selfish. I love you.'

I feel sorry for him. He's never cried like this before. I return to the marriage bed under the oak beams. The moon is shining through a gap in the curtains, falling across the white carpet.

'Let's make love in the moonlight.' He throws the doona back and pulls me out of bed onto the floor with him.

As he slides in and out of me, I count the thrusts and focus on the moonlight through a gap in the curtains. It doesn't take long.

Back in bed, he holds me close and says, 'I have nightmares about you leaving, of not seeing you or the girls again.'

'Robert, can we wait to talk some more when you come back from Germany? I promise I won't see Derek again, and I'll still be here when you come back.'

I hold him until he falls asleep. I turn on my side, trying to imagine life going on with him. Perhaps we'll go back to how we were, living separate/together lives, parenting the children. Perhaps I can start studying again or find something to occupy my mind. Perhaps he will spend more time with us, and I won't feel so alone.

As I lie, unable to go back to sleep, I wonder whether he's really had a change of heart. He's lost the detachment that I've seen growing in him in the last couple of years since that affair with Marie and the birth of Penelope. He used to play with them a lot, making up funny stories, chanting to them in a sing-song voice. He was lovely with them when they were babies. In Sydney, in our harbourside flat, he was the only one who could get Sophia to sleep at night by lying her across his tummy when she was having a fit of colic. In England, one evening when I was breastfeeding Caitlin, Sophia was playing on the floor and didn't want to go to bed. He pulled her up from the floor to get her ready for bed and dislocated her arm. He was so upset, he rushed out to our neighbour, who drove them to hospital to get her arm put back in.

He was the one who cuddled Caitlin back to sleep when she cried to be picked up from her cot after her stint in hospital with croup, or later when she climbed out of bed and came into ours. She would climb in between us and wriggle, and I couldn't get back to sleep, so I'd go to sleep in her bed. In the morning, I'd find her snuggled into his back.

The first day after I came home from hospital with Penelope, I was bathing her in the baby bath in our bedroom. I'd put Caitlin and Sophia in the big bath. Caitlin, warm and dripping, came to me, and when she saw Penelope in my arms, she ran away from me, calling, 'Daddy!' She tripped on her towel and fell down the stairs, puncturing her forehead on a screw on the heater vent at the foot of the stairs. Robert called our neighbour again, who drove them to hospital so he could hold her in the car. He brought her home with stitches in her forehead.

He would take Penelope on his knee when she was having a tantrum, singing to her and soothing her. He would rock her in his arms and walk her round her little attic bedroom, put her in her cot, and when she started to cry again, he'd go through the ritual again. Now, he jokes that when she wouldn't stop crying, he'd put her in the spare room and close the door. But I don't remember that. I think she was lonely up in the attic, and I think we should have brought her down to our bedroom. He wanted the bedroom to be just for us. I wish I had insisted on having her near us. I would have kept her beside me until she was ready to sleep with her sisters.

He loves them so much, they mean the world to him, I know. It's just that he puts them out of his mind when he's working. He relies on me to hold them, love them, look after them, comfort them when he can't be there.

He comes in to the spare room the day before he goes to Germany, a bunch of jonquils in his hand. 'I know you love these. They're the first of the season.'

'Oh, Robert, how thoughtful of you. I do! There are only snowdrops out in our garden so far.' I inhale their heady fragrance – pungent spice and bitter orange.

Next day, I help him pack and we have a special morning tea, with scones and jam and cream. The girls cluster round him and he sings them nursery rhymes and plays their favourite game, one he made up, about the wibbly wobbly family. He takes each of them on his knee in turn, chanting with them,

> Wibbly wobbly, wibbly wobbly, off we wibble to wobbly land,
> wobbly wibbly, wobbly wibbly, back to wibbly wobbly home.

He kisses each of them and says in his normal voice, 'Darlings, I'll be home again before you can say wibbly wobbly ten times without stopping!'

They cluster round him, giggling, kissing him and snuggling up to him.

I can't break this.

Six

While he is away, Robert sends me a pink rose every day accompanied by one word, each adding up to a sentence. So far, it reads, 'Forgive me.'

I don't know what to make of this, it is so unlike him.

On the third day, a postcard comes, with a picture of rambling roses growing over a brick wall and cottage with a thatched roof. On the back of it, he has scribbled a message: 'Rose, be mine, and I'll love you with all my heart.'

'Dear Robert,' I write,

> You are taking me by storm! First a flower each day, and this morning a postcard. I'm sorry I missed waving to you – you turned away as the taxi backed out of the driveway, and I went to the kitchen window, but you were gone. The second flower came yesterday, a perfect pink rose, with leaves and fern. I have put it in a brown Benedictine bottle, with the pink ribbon tied behind the neck. I wish you could see it.
>
> Fancy falling in love with your wife after twelve years of marriage! It rather frightens me – I'm afraid of not being able to return your passion. We've never really had mutual passion before, have we? In the past it's always been so evanescent – here one day, gone the next... And the last couple of years, you've been buried in your work most of the time.
>
> Another rose has arrived. Am I to have one every day? How romantic. A month ago, I wouldn't have believed you capable of such exotic gestures.

I try to resume my normal life once I finish marking the papers. I am overeating; my weight has gone up to nearly nine stone again from eight and a half. I am lethargic. There are a thousand and one jobs to do – notes for the playgroup, of which I am secretary, letters, sewing, clearing out cupboards. I have no heart for decorating or house improvement any more, and I feel temporary in the farmhouse. I fret over all the jobs that need to be done but don't feel like doing them. My life is emptier than ever, except for the children.

This morning, as well as another rose, there was a letter from him, a couple of scrawled pages with the imprint of a Frankfurt hotel.

'I still haven't got back my equilibrium,' he writes, 'but I managed to give my paper without breaking down. I was afraid of stammering and no words coming out. I've never felt like this before.'

I stand at the cupboard in the girls' room, trying to sort through their clothes and pick out the ones they've grown out of. My heart is not in it. The house feels emptier than it ever has. He says in the letter that he has decided we will return to Australia as soon as we can sell the house. I'm in shock. I had no idea he would do this.

Mrs Green, my housekeeper, has taken Penelope out on a walk to the village shops to get some bread and milk. Sophia and Caitlin are at school. Caitlin started there in May, after she turned four. The first morning, I stayed with her for the first half hour or so. She cried when I left her, but by the time I picked them up, she was happy, dancing round me, telling me all the fun things she'd done. It's a lovely school, with family grouping, so the little ones and older ones are in a mixed class, and the rooms are organised in activity centres. They move round in small groups during the day, from reading, to writing, to crafts, to numbers, and so on. She and Sophia won't be there when she turns five. Where will they be? At a school in Australia, or somewhere in the States, or in Europe?

I pull out Caitlin's clothes from last summer and put them in an op-shop bag. She's grown out of them already. She's going to be taller than Sophia. Outside, spring is here, and the horse chestnut trees are cloaked in clusters of pale green leaves bursting out of their shiny maroon buds. We probably won't be here when they are in full flower. Robert says he's taken advice on selling the house, and it will sell quickly because it's in such a good position, on a half-acre of land, and has been partly restored. He must have talked to someone about it before he went to Germany.

How can he do this, out of the blue, without discussing it with me? I suppose he doesn't think I have a say in it. I didn't dream he would sell up and quit his job. He's loved the work here, his role, and he loves living in England and being able to hop over to the Continent on work trips or for the occasional family holiday. I thought he'd have another year at least at the laboratory before he gets his system running the way he wants it to. I don't want to leave here, I don't want to leave this house, I don't want to leave England. It's so like him to present me with a fait accompli, no discussion. He's used to getting his own way. He is the eldest of three brothers, and his youngest brother, who was his groomsman at our wedding, told me that he always manipulated his parents and brothers so that he got what he wanted. Neither of his brothers have his intelligence, ambition, and drive, and in many ways, they are nicer people.

I've felt more at home here than I have since I was a small child on an isolated farm in the outback. The children and I are luggage that he can pack up and take with him wherever he wants to be. I have no hope I can persuade him to stay, and I have no power, because he is the income earner and the house is in his name.

Until now, I still had a hope of being with Derek. I think he let Marion take over because she threatened him in some way…maybe he was afraid of what she would do. If we leave here, I know I'll never see him again. I had a hope that somehow, down the track, he and she would agree to separate, and I could persuade Robert to agree to a separation with liberal access for him to the children. I can't imagine living with Robert till our girls grow up. We have so little in common, and although he professes now to love me, it is conditional. Conditional on me responding to him and having sex with him when he wants it. My body will be licensed to him and he will pursue his career and travel when and where he wants to, to 'provide a roof over our heads and give the girls a good education'. These were the words he spoke to me when we last talked about the future.

*

He's back from Germany. When the girls are in bed, he starts to talk about going back to Australia. We sit in the living room in separate chairs, and I pick up my knitting so I have something to focus on, to keep my hands busy, to help me talk about risky subjects.

I start with the safe and obvious. 'How did your paper go?' I say, checking the pattern to see where I'm up to.

'Really well. Several people came up to me before I gave it and said they'd heard about my work…they wanted to know more. So that gave me a good start. I got right into the swing of it. I didn't stammer or break down.'

'That's interesting,' I say, 'that you lost your stammer when you were performing.'

'Well, I'm used to public speaking, I enjoy it. And the paper was on the work I've done here, which is ground-breaking.'

'So did you get a good response to it?'

'Sure. Several people approached me afterwards and sounded me out about consulting for their set-ups or doing a visiting fellowship there…one in Switzerland, one in US, one in Belgium.'

More trips, more absences! I wonder what he has in mind, beyond leaving here and going back home for a while. He plans ahead, but he doesn't usually tell me what he's planning. I need to know what he's thinking.

I start a new row of knitting and take a deep breath. 'Why do you want to go back home, Robert?'

He stands up and starts pacing back and forth in front of me. 'Because I know you and Derek won't stick to our agreement. You'll begin to meet again – you'll leave me to live with him. You'll take my children away.' His voice rises to a higher pitch, and he's trembling. He moves over to the bar.

I don't know what to say. I need to stay calm. Knit one, purl two, knit one, purl two.

'I'll lose my daughters to a man who's a loser,' he says, pouring a whisky from his latest duty-free purchases.

This stings me. Derek is working hard to build his business and support his family. 'That's not fair, Robert. He doesn't have a career, like you, and a salary, but he's talented and he's doing his best to create a sustainable income.'

'He's a loser! He's idealistic, impractical. I'm building a world reputation – that takes hard work and sacrifice. I know I've been absent a lot. But I want to make up for it.' He turns back towards me.

'How will you do that, if you're building an international career?'

'I'll find a better position, one that pays more and gives me more freedom to follow my own ideas.'

I put my knitting down and look up at him. 'Ever since I've known you, you've put your work first. First it was your thesis and your students, now it's your system and your reputation. You've been away so much, the girls hardly notice when you're not here.'

'I know that. I want to make up for it.' He calms down and moves over near my chair. 'That's why I want to take a break, so we can spend time together. I don't know how much time I'll have. I don't expect to grow old. I reckon I'll be dead before I'm fifty.' He's pacing back and forth again.

'You seem pretty healthy to me.' I check the pattern to see if it's time to decrease for the armholes.

'I was a sickly child. The doctor told my mother I had a delicate constitution. I couldn't play sport, so she bought me a chemistry set. I nearly blew the house up one day.' He chuckles. 'I was doing an experiment under the house, and it blew up in my face. I lost the sight of my right eye for a while, but it came back.'

I've heard this story before. His eye still waters when he's tired. He smokes, and drinks a lot, at least in the evenings, and he doesn't exercise. But apart from getting indigestion when he eats too much fat or pizza with anchovies, he seems pretty robust.

'Maybe you've grown out of that! You've been healthy while we've been together.'

'Hmm, well, what's happened now has really thrown me, and it's made me realise…' He pauses in front of me again. 'I want to make the most of life, to be the father and husband you need, to enjoy seeing my daughters grow older. I know I've put my career first, but I'm well known now, I've made a name for myself…everyone at the conference knew who I was before I gave my paper.'

'That must have been very reassuring,' I say, wondering where this is leading. Is he really going to change, or is this just a fit of the wobbles and he'll go back to how he was? 'But why do you want to go back to Australia? When we left there, you said it was too small a pond for you, you needed more scope.'

'I'm just… I need to be near my family. We can get a holiday unit at a beach outside town, we can spend more time together. And I'll have time to look for another job. I want a tenured position in a good university.' He sits down and drains his glass.

Back 'home'. With his family. I think of the farewell party his parents threw for us before we left Australia. It was under the house, with a keg and a barbecue. The men stood around the keg drinking and the women sat in a semicircle talking about their kids, the price of meat, the beach house that a son-in-law had bought… I made an excuse and went upstairs to check on Sophia. I had to feed her, I said. I sat and held her and cried.

'My parents stuck together through everything. Dad always put the family first, and Mum devoted herself to looking after us all.'

This is the model of family life he aspires to, one of solidity, success and permanence, and he believes we can make such a life, if only I can get over this immature desire I have for the perfect love.

'There's no such thing as the perfect love,' he says, as if he's read my thoughts. He gets up and stands behind my chair. 'Before I met you, I thought I'd met the love of my life. But she was a Catholic, and she wouldn't marry me because she wanted me to convert, and I couldn't hack the thought of bringing our kids up as Catholics.'

I thought I'd met the love of my life when Derek walked into it. But he came too late. He made promises he couldn't keep, and the dreams we spun together dissolved overnight. Perhaps he also saw that he had a family, children and a wife who needed him, and wants to make it work. Perhaps he is wiser than I am. I seem to be the only one who is still holding on to the impossible.

I suspect that Robert is more afraid of losing the children than he is of losing me. But he can't separate them from me.

He walks over to the fireplace, then back towards me. He stares at me for a minute, then says, his voice rising, 'If you go with him and I die, you'll give all I've worked so hard for to Derek. He'll squander it on his business that's not going anywhere, and you and the children will be paupers.'

I wonder if he really is losing his reason. He seems to have plotted it all out and built a scenario to justify uprooting us. I can't get through to him when he's like this. I need to close this conversation.

'I'm going to bed early,' I say, as he pours another drink. 'I'll sleep in the spare room, just for tonight. I've got a headache.' I push the stitches back along the needles and fold the knitting up.

I lie in the single bed, trying to breathe out the tension. But my thoughts won't switch off. I think back over the steps I've taken, and I realise how much I've put at risk by letting myself fall in love. When I thought of leaving Robert for Derek, I didn't think through the consequences for the children; I was preoccupied with my own need for love. I persuaded myself they wouldn't miss him, they'd probably see as much of him if they were separated as they did when we lived together. Now, seeing how devastated he is, struggling to restore himself to a central place in their lives and mine, I realise I can't take them from him. I remember how it felt to live without a father. I don't want my children to go through that. So far, they don't seem to have been affected. Their life has gone on in the normal patterns, and because Robert's been away a lot, I don't think they've picked up on the tensions between us.

Tomorrow is another day. I'll try to find a rapport with him, so that we can talk about the future without falling through the ice.

Next evening, when the girls are watching a favourite serial before bed, he and I sit at the table.

'Robert, are you serious about selling up here and going back to Australia?'

'Yep. I want a break from here. I've been held back by a tight budget. The managers don't realise that they need to put money into a world-class computer system to keep ahead of the game in atomic energy. I've had to work overtime to get things done, because they haven't given me enough staff. I want some time to think and decide on the next step in my career. And I want to spend some time with you and the girls while they're little. They'll grow up fast enough.'

I can't imagine our relationship will be different except that he'll be around more, and when he is, he'll want more sex. The more I'm attractive to other men, the more he wants me. Yesterday, he gave me some leather gear he bought in Germany – a G-string, fringed miniskirt, midriff top and long fringed boots. I love the fringed miniskirt and the boots, but I can't imagine wearing the G-string and midriff top. They might have looked OK before I had three kids, but there's a pillow round my tummy and I have stretch marks. Maybe he was thinking of the girl in New York who's skinnier than me and hasn't had children. Why does he want me to wear them? So he can think of her while he's having sex with me? Or maybe he met some pretty young German girl while he was in Frankfurt. He wouldn't tell me if he had, because he wants to get back in with me, he wants to take me away from here, from our home, from the man over the road. He wants to take me back to where he feels safe.

I put the G-string and top away in my drawer. I'll take them to the op shop, I'm not going to wear them. I try the skirt on…it fits OK, and looks good with the boots, which fit me. I won't be able to wear them in Australia, though. Women dress differently here, more daring. Miniskirts and boots topped by maxi-coats are the thing in winter. And the longer your legs, the better. Mine aren't long, but the boots give the illusion of length.

But the gift bothers me. I know it has strings attached. Apart from the black jumpsuit (my hooker outfit, his penance for the affair with the New York girl), he's never given me anything like this.

I think I'd rather have rosebuds. That romance of calling me his rose was so out of character for him. He doesn't tell me what his sexual fantasies are, but this outfit tells me more than words can.

When the children are asleep, he asks me to dress up. Perhaps he will calm down and go back to his normal patterns if I try to satisfy his needs. This too will pass.

'Come downstairs when you're ready,' he says.

I put on the dark green suede skirt and the boots, and a tight ribbed white top.

'Wh-whew!' he whistles when I walk down the stairs. He's in the sitting room with the peeling wallpaper. He's turned the main light off, leaving a small table lamp on, and set up a polaroid camera on the Cotswold stone bar that Derek was so scathing about the first time he visited the house.

'Where's the top and G-string?' he says, as he steps behind the bar.

'Oh…they don't fit. I've put on weight.'

'That's OK, I like curves.' His eyes flick over my figure. He turns to the bar and pours two glasses of cognac. He hands one to me and goes into the living room.

I sit on the only decent chair in the room and sip from my brandy balloon, wondering what Derek is doing. He's probably at the mill trying to get an order finished, shavings around his feet, hands filmed with sawdust. A different world, a world of physical work, shaping wood into desirable objects for families; hands that are strong and calloused, yet soft and gentle.

Robert returns from the living room with some large cushions and throws them on the floor. He removes his shoes and settles down on one of the cushions with his drink, patting the one beside him. 'Come on! You look gorgeous. I'd like to try something new for a change. Let's pretend….' He produces some knotted leather thongs from his pocket, then starts loosening his clothing, undoing buttons and zippers. He gestures to me to take my top and bra off. 'Leave your boots and skirt on. I'll do the rest.' He hands me the thongs. 'Here, hold these for me.'

*

It's morning. For a moment, I don't know where I am. Oak beams above me... I can't remember coming upstairs. I remember him handing me leather thongs, but what happened after that is a blank. I guess we had more cognac – did he spike my drink? There's a bitter, burnt taste in my mouth. Maybe I smoked some of his cigar. My head is throbbing, I just want to go back to sleep. He is sleeping heavily bedside me in the bed, naked. I look at his body, curled up in a foetal position. There are red marks around his buttocks. Did I do that?

I wish he would not wake up. I turn over and face the window, listening to the girls playing in their bedroom. I wish I wasn't here. I wish I were a child again, hadn't grown up, had sex, got married. But then... I wouldn't have my daughters.

I try to think ahead and all I can see is more of the same. I have to get through this day, and tomorrow, and tomorrow, and act as if we are a normal couple who love each other and have three young daughters and a future together.

There's no one I can talk to about it. English women are very reserved about their private lives, and since we moved out to the farmhouse, we mainly see our friends at dinner parties and dances. I'm a good hostess, and Robert loves dancing and talking, and for all they know, we are the perfect couple. I don't know what their private lives are like, and they don't know that he has affairs and I've fallen in love with the man across the road. Maybe they have kinky sex too. Maybe they have affairs. Flirting at parties is de rigueur, but if they go further, they don't talk about it. Derek's the only one I've shared my secrets with, and he is lost to me.

Seven

I bump into Derek in the village one day, not long after the leather thong evening.

'Anna,' he says, taking my hands. 'I…please forgive me for what happened.'

'Why didn't you speak to me yourself,' I say, pulling my hands away. 'At least you could have seen me in private, not let her speak for you and say nothing, sitting there like a zombie.' My voice is shaking. All the grief and anger I'd locked up after that day he and Marion came over floods up into my chest and throat.

'I'm sorry. I wanted to. But she forced me to stay away.'

'How did she do that?'

'The day before, when I told her how I feel about you, she grabbed a kitchen knife and tried to attack me, then turned it on herself. I managed to take it from her before she could cut herself. We're both on tranquillisers. I thought I could get through this, but seeing you today, how pale you are, how much I've hurt you, I think it's just the drugs that numbed me.'

I stare at his face. His hair is dishevelled and his eyes are bloodshot. I can't think of anything to say.

'I don't know what will happen, but I have to stay with her for now. I can't leave her…it's not safe!' he pleads, clutching my hand again.

'There's no point, Derek. We can't ever be together. Robert's decided we're going back to Australia. He's putting the house on the market tomorrow.'

He stands there, looking lost. 'I still love you, I always will.'

'I'll have to go,' I say. 'Robert will be back soon. He won't leave me alone for long. He thinks you and I will get together again if we have a chance.'

'Don't give up on me!' he calls as I walk away.

I decide to go and see Dr Greenaway, the same GP as Derek and Marion see. He's already heard the story from them or, most likely, from Marion. Derek wouldn't be honest about his feelings in front of her. I need to talk to someone. Perhaps he can refer me for counselling.

'Are you sleeping OK?' he asks, after he's taken my pulse and blood pressure.

'Not much, not when Robert's there. I can't remember when I last had a good night's sleep.'

'I'll give you a script for a mild sedative. It should help you relax and get to sleep. I think it would be a good idea to talk to someone about what's happened and where you want to go from here. I'll suggest that to your husband too. Ask him to come and see me.'

I recall that Robert has been to see him already and told him I'm frigid. Then bought me a massager. I haven't told Dr Greenaway much about our marriage, except that Robert's away more than he's home, and that he's told me of a couple of affairs he's had on his trips. He refers me to Dr FitzWilliam, who is head of the psych unit at the Nuffield Hospital in Oxford. I don't expect a psych doctor can help me, given my last experience with his profession, after Robert had the affair with Maureen. I picture myself sitting again in a room with a man who is looking for symptoms of a psychiatric disorder in me, probably with a couple of students observing.

I had hoped we could have marriage counselling, but on the National Health, apparently, this is all that is on offer.

Robert doesn't believe in counselling. 'Why would you go and talk about your private life to some stranger? What do they know about what makes a good marriage?' He thinks all that is wrong is that he's been away from home too much and been too absorbed in his work, and that I'm frigid and immature. 'You haven't grown up!' he said to me when I tried to tell him how lonely I am. 'You've read too many stories about the perfect love. You still believe in the fairies at the bottom of the garden. The only way to make things happen is to work for them.'

I have a few sessions with Dr FitzWilliam. He is an elderly man with a large paunch, pince-nez, and thinning hair. He seems like someone from my grandparents' time. Not that I ever knew them – they were all dead before I was born.

As he listens to me talk about my marriage and how empty it has become, how trapped I feel, his hand steals up to his nose and begins to explore its cavities with practised finger, corkscrewing energetically, while his eyes glaze over as if this were a meditative practice. Zen and the art of nose-picking. It's gross, and I feel like leaving, but I know then he'll just find a label for me and write me off. I don't want to see a psychiatrist, I'm not crazy, I'm just unhappy. But there's no one else to talk to.

At last, he sighs, withdraws his finger, folds his arms and allows his eyes to close, his mouth to fall open as he sinks into sleep. I sit and wait for him to wake up, wondering how long he will sleep, whether he will help me when he does. He wakes after a few moments and asks me a question as if I'd just finished speaking.

Dr FitzWilliam sees Robert separately a couple of times, but Robert won't tell me anything about the sessions. In my last session with him, he tells me that it is time I grow up.

'Your husband tells me you had a solitary childhood and you lived in an imaginary world, acting out stories of undying love and romance, with fairies and magical beings.'

It wasn't quite like that, but I'm not going to argue with him. I grew up overnight when my father left.

He pauses and closes his eyes. Is he going to sleep again?

He opens them and looks at me from under his shaggy white brows, over the top of his half-lenses. 'Being a Christian, my dear, means accepting that you can't always have what you want.'

I'm not a Christian!

'By accepting your responsibilities instead of trying to escape them, you will become a stronger, better person. Your husband,' he intones, 'is like you in one respect. He lives in a castle with a moat around it.

You live in another one. What you need to do is cross the bridge, join him in the castle he has built for you.'

I think I understand what he means. It is true, Robert has built our domestic castle, and works hard to maintain the edifice. But I live in it too, the housewife, mother and hostess. I am also a prisoner in it. There is a moat and a drawbridge. But Derek stole across it when Robert was away, and nothing will ever be the same again. Perhaps when he says I live in another castle, he means my castle in the air, my dreams of a mutual, equal love.

I go back to Dr Greenaway to report on my sessions and have him check my IUD, which has been giving me some discomfort since the leather thong session with Robert. I look at my file while he is out of the room, getting some forms for a referral for an IUD refitting. At the top of my file, there's a letter from Dr FitzWilliam.

> This woman is a perfectionist idealist. To her, the grass in the next field will always be greener. The best therapy for her is to teach her that the husband she has is the best husband she's got.

Eight

I see Derek a couple more times. One wet Sunday when Robert is at work, ironing out some bugs in the system, I feel overwhelmed by the need to see him, and leave the children playing at a friend's house. I drive out to his workshop at the old mill and walk up the winding stairs to the work room. I freeze in the doorway. Derek and Marion stand together by the lathe, planing a piece of wood. Marion places the plane at the edge of the plank and presses forwards along the surface. Derek then takes it from her and checks it with his fingers, feeling for uneven patches. They have their backs to me, and with the background noise of the machinery, they don't hear me. I turn and walk softly down the stairs and drive away like a thief, hoping they haven't seen my car through the window. I should have known she'd be here with him. She often works with him when they have a deadline for an order. As I pull out onto the roadway, I scold myself for giving in to my impulse. They are a couple struggling to make a living, with three young children. Derek and I shared a brief fantasy of a life together, and it was never going to happen.

In the last days at Walnut Tree Farmhouse, one clear February night, I step out through the back door. Snow has fallen during the day. All is still; my feet crunch on the powdery carpet that shines blue-white in the moonlight. The air is so cold my eyes sting. I move past the crab apple tree veiled in white towards the chook house. I want to check the gate is shut properly and the chooks are safe from foxes. A tall shadow steps out from behind the iron shelter.

'Who is it?' My heart thumps against my ribs.

'It's me, love. Sorry, did I frighten you?'

'Derek! I thought you were the marsh murderer! What are you doing here?'

'I had to see you. Since I bumped into you in the village, and you told me you're going back to Australia, I haven't been able to think of anything else.' He moves towards me, taking off his glasses, and folds his arms around me, sinking his face into my neck. His duffle coat toggles press into the soft flesh of my breasts.

'You're mad. Where's Marion?'

'At home. I've been working late at the mill, getting a consignment order ready. Work's the only thing that's kept me going. Before I bumped into you again, I kidded myself I was OK, but I think it was only the tranquillisers. Anna…'

'Yes?' I begin to relax into his warmth, feeling the closeness of his body melt away some of the tension that has built up in me in the last month.

'When I saw you looking so pale and sad, I could have killed myself for causing you so much pain. I'm sorry. When are you leaving?'

'Soon. We've sold the house, we just have to pack up.'

'No matter where you go, what part of the world you live in – I'll always love you. My Anna… I'll come and find you one day, and we can be together.'

I push his face away. My glasses have misted over from the warmth of his body, so I take them off and put them in my cardigan pocket. I can't see into his eyes. 'It won't work. You're not free now, how will it be any different in the future? How do you know I'll ever be free? I think we only had one chance, and we've lost it.'

'I don't know – I just can't bear the thought of never seeing you again. Let me feel you once more.'

'No! It's late, it's below freezing, Robert will be home any minute…'

'It's not lust I feel for you, you know. Give me a few moments to remember you by.' He slides his hand up under my long skirt and pulls down my woollen tights and pants. His mouth burrows under my jumper and finds my breasts.

For him, loving me means having sex with me. It's all he can think of; not that we'll never see each other again, all the inner parts of our minds and hearts we've shared, the tender, lost places…just feeling me, knowing my body in any way he can steal so he can remember me when I'm gone. He and Robert are alike in this, but his hands and mouth are tender and his heart is open. He doesn't calculate like Robert does, he just feels.

My body is responding, but my mind is whirring with thoughts like, 'What if Robert comes? What if one of the girls wakes up and cries and I'm not there?' After a few moments, I push his hand away and pull his face up from my breast.

An owl calls with a mournful note from the old walnut tree in the neighbouring field. I kiss Derek and hold his face for a moment, then run towards the house. I turn at the door. I can just see his tall shape outlined against the moonlit field and the fence. The owl calls again, then flies from the walnut tree, its wings dark shadows against the circle of the moon.

Nine

Our possessions are all packed. I'm allowed to fill one tea chest with household things I want to keep. In it go gifts from my mother – the cream pottery lamp base, the raw wool lampshade, the woven woollen table mats, the carved wooden Noah's Ark set, the fairy forest with witches and maidens, a dragon, a fairy king and queen and foresters – all presents she delighted in finding for us on her last visit. Some embroidered cushion covers, watercolour paintings of the farmhouse and of Saint Helen's medieval church in Abingdon that an artist friend painted for us…little bits of England. I think to myself as I pack that I won't have a settled home like this again. I suspect there'll be a lot more moves in my life. But a few precious things can furnish a home anywhere.

The furniture is sold to locals and to dealers, I've sold off nearly all my books, going back to my undergraduate days, for sixpence apiece, and culled our clothes. It breaks my heart to do all this. I had imagined that we would live here till the girls were older, maybe even teenagers. All those plans we had for the house – doing up the sitting room, renovating the spare bedroom and the kitchen, opening up the second attic – were just dreams. There was a time when Robert shared them, but over the past year or so, he's been somewhere else. Where will our next home be? Nothing can replace this, my share of England, under licence for a while. I felt at home here, nurtured by the climate and the culture, accepted by our friends. Two of our daughters were born here. I will return some day, perhaps. But I can't imagine coming back with Robert.

He has planned a little goodbye holiday for us, first in the Lake District, then in London. Perhaps he remembers me saying I'd love to go back to the Lakes when he went to his conference up there. On our brief Cook's tour of northern England and Scotland, when Sophia was three and Caitlin a baby, I loved the cloudy skies, the misty valleys, the shadowed mountains mirrored in the lakes, the grey stone walls and cottages, the shingled rooftops, and longed to spend more time there, to immerse myself in this tranquil, lovely place. Now I have my chance, but our two days and nights here are claustrophobic. It rains all day, so we can't do much walking, just keep the girls amused with board games, stories, indoor hide-and-seek, cookie-making, and cartoons.

When they are asleep at night, Robert gets me to sit on his knee. He hasn't mentioned the leather thongs or asked me to dress up again. Perhaps he's read something in that sex book he got for me (I haven't read it!) about foreplay. His idea of foreplay has always been rudimentary, but now it's digital penetration. His finger inside me reminds me of Dr FitzWilliam and his corkscrewing of his nose. When we go to bed, there is the usual thrusting and groaning, thankfully fairly short-lived. Sex with him has always been noisy and brief.

This morning, on another misty South Lakes day, I woke up with sharp pains in my uterus and there was blood on the sheet. Robert takes me to a doctor in the nearest town, Bowness-on-Windermere. Dr Brook is an older man, with shaggy grey hair, bristling brows and deep smile lines. I feel comfortable with him and wonder how much I can tell him. I describe the pain and the bleeding. He looks concerned and asks me to get on the couch so he can examine me.

'Hmmm. Your IUD is dislodged. I'll have to remove it. You need to ask your husband to refrain, to allow the uterus to heal. Has he been …rough with you lately, when making love?'

'Well, not exactly, but he's been very vigorous in…foreplay. I did get a referral from our GP to have a new one fitted before this happened. It's been uncomfortable for a while, but I just haven't had time to see about it.' The night of the thongs started it.

He asks me some more questions, and I tell him about our near break-up, and Robert's decision to take the family back to Australia, to save the marriage.

'You have three children, is that right? Do you want any more?'

'I don't, but I know he wants a boy.'

'Ah.' He turns to remove his gloves.

When we are sitting at his desk again, he pauses and looks at me, as if trying to find the right words. 'Mrs Anderson, your husband may want to displace your IUD so that you will get pregnant again. Unconsciously, I mean. Perhaps, if you'll pardon me interpreting the feelings of someone I don't know, to tie you to him. Since, as you say, he is afraid of losing you.'

I look up in surprise. I meet his kind, grey eyes.

'Perhaps you're right, doctor. He knows I don't love him. But I've agreed to stay with him because…because I don't want to hurt him any more than I already have, and because of the children. So I'm just hoping I can…kind of…get used to it and make something of our life together. And I know that means having a sexual relationship with him. Perhaps that will get better for me; perhaps he will settle down and become less anxious, once we've left England.'

'In that case, I can prescribe the pill for you.'

'But I stopped taking it because of scares about it causing blood clots.'

'Yes, that's true, but there's a brand with a lower hormone dose now; and taking it for a short term, say three months, shouldn't have any ill effects. Then, should you need it,' (he looks at me with a question in his eyes) 'you can get another IUD fitted.'

I know what the question is, and I can't answer it. If we're still together? My heart contracts, my mind goes blank.

I walk out with a prescription for the pill and an antibiotic course and go to the pharmacy before I meet Robert. He's taken the children to a little tea shop to have a treat.

*

Our last days in England are spent in London. Because of Robert's work and our young children, so far, we've only had the occasional visit for shopping or the theatre.

We stay in a comfortable family hotel in Kensington, in a street lined with symmetrical Georgian two- and three-storey buildings, with small courtyards enclosed in black wrought-iron fences, embroidered with hedges. The bus goes past the door, and it's a ten-minute walk to the tube station. But apart from a ride in a red double-decker bus at the girls' request, Robert decides to treat us to the traditional London black cabs.

We have a wonderful lunch that stretches on through the afternoon at Veeraswamy's, London's oldest Indian restaurant. Gold and red, silver and crystal, starched white tablecloths, glittering chandeliers, waiters in traditional Raj-style dress, and, to the children's delight, little stuffed velvet elephants, beaded and embroidered, that they can sit on. The meal is rich with many courses, and the *pièce de résistance* is a silver epergne, with a large central dish holding creamy yellow dahl, and many branching dishes filled with different chutneys, poppadums, fruit, coconut, and naan bread.

Robert announced, before we left the farmhouse, that he wanted the girls to have their own passports. 'It's not fair they should be on yours,' he said, narrowing his eyes.

I can't think of an answer to this but, as always, I'm sure he has an ulterior motive. He got me to sign a statutory declaration that I consented to separate passports for the girls, and submitted it with the passport application.

He still doesn't trust me. He watches me closely when we go out together. Yesterday, I said I wanted to walk down to the nearest post box to post a letter to Mum. I could see from the way he looked at me that he thought it was a letter to Derek. It was. I'd agreed to write to Derek, and to set up a private postbox when we settled in Australia. I don't believe we'll ever see each other again, but Derek wants to hold onto this fragile connection between us, and at least I can write to him about my feelings.

Time was tight with the passport application, so Robert arranged to pick them up from the GPO in London. While he's doing that, I treat myself and the girls to summer outfits and underwear at Marks and Spencer, and we get a cab to Knightsbridge to have high tea at Harrods. I find myself humming, 'Maybe it's because I'm a Londoner, that I love London so!'

London works a little magic on Robert and me. We can't have sex because my uterus is still healing, but I fellate him. It's an art I practised when we first started dating, using it at times that were unsafe for me to have intercourse. I don't mind doing it, as I don't feel so invaded, and he comes easily. I can detach myself and he is always affectionate afterwards. We are softer with each other, he is gentler, less needy and demanding, and I feel like a princess, being treated to all these elegant delights. I begin to hope that we can find a place somewhere where we can make a life together, make more friends, bring our girls up, be separately creative and share a happy home.

Ten

The Qantas Boeing 747, which, Robert proudly tells me, has revolutionised long flights, makes two stops, Bahrain and Singapore. The girls are goggle-eyed at first; Sophia was only three months old when we flew to England from Australia, with several stops on the way; and she and Caitlin don't remember their flights to and from the USA when Caitlin was only three. As for Penelope, she's never been on a plane before, except in my uterus on that awful trip after Robert told me about his affair with Marie.

The novelty soon wears off for them, and they alternate between sleeping, squabbling and watching the movies shown on the screens that descend from the ceiling between the aisles. Robert and I don't talk much; he reads computer science journals when he isn't watching a movie, and I read *Mister Men* books to the girls and arbitrate their squabbles, take them to the toilet, help them with the airplane food, distract them with the little puzzles and games I packed.

I can't sleep on planes, so when the girls are asleep, I read *The Group* by Mary McCarthy. It's interesting because, although it's about a group of 1930s American college graduates, it could be about me. These women struggle with breastfeeding a new baby, have premarital sex or unsatisfying or messy sex, worry about contraception, believe in romantic love, submit to their husbands' desires and demands. The men in the book, save one, are overbearing, unfaithful, completely absent from their marriages, and bastards. Forty years on, I and probably many other women are still living in unequal marriages, trying to conform to what is expected of them, yearning for fulfilment. *The Group* was banned in Australia when it came out in 1963 because of the explicit sex scenes. I'd been married to Robert for three years then, and sex was definitely a dud as far as I was concerned. The difference between me and *The*

Group women is that they had each other to share their conflicts and desires with. I had no one in England I could talk to about my difficulties with Robert, apart from Derek, too little and too late, and there's no one in Australia that I know that I can talk to about it either. I can't see a way out of the mess that I'm in.

At last, after another flight from Brisbane to Mackay on a much smaller plane, a Fokker Friendship, we arrive. Robert has arranged for us to stay the first night with his parents. They meet us at the airport, waving to us as we cross the tarmac. To the girls, they are strangers, but they soon warm up to their granddad, tall and wiry, with short stubbled silver hair and kind grey eyes behind his glasses. He scoops Penelope up in his arms and, to my surprise, she snuggles in happily. Normally she is wary with strangers. Their grandmother takes Caitlin and Sophia by the hands and walks slowly with them towards the car park, listening to their chatter about the plane trip.

We sit at the table with 'Mum' and 'Dad' – as they want me to call them – and make small talk.

Dad tells Robert about the unit he's found for us. 'It's at Eimio Beach, fifteen minutes' drive north off the Bruce Highway. You'll love it. Nice sheltered bay, powder-soft sand, safe swimming for the kids. The unit's furnished, a standalone near the beach, so you'll have privacy. And we found a car for you…an old Vauxhall station wagon, a few miles on the clock, but it's in good nick.'

Mum goes into the kitchen to serve lunch, and I follow her. I don't feel comfortable calling this other woman Mum. To myself, I call her Lorna. I've never felt at home with her, this plain, wide-hipped woman who gave up her job as a schoolteacher to look after her husband and three boys, who goes to church on Sundays and cooks meat and three veg for dinner. Lunch is cold corned beef with a lettuce leaf, potato salad and tinned beetroot. And sliced white bread, already buttered. She shows me how to make the salad dressing – a thick cream made from tinned Carnation milk whipped with sugar and vinegar.

She's wearing a cotton floral dress with buttoned bodice, a belt around her broad waist, and a gathered skirt. And flat-heeled comfortable shoes. Her only concession to vanity is to wear lipstick and eau de cologne and to have her white hair permed every three months, so it frames her wide face with tight, frizzy curls.

The only thing I like about her appearance is her eyes, a warmer blue than Robert's, almost the colour of the cornflowers my father loved to grow.

But she is phlegmatic and reserved, stolid and sensible, all the things I don't want to be. I like Dad better. He's jolly and kind-hearted, and has a raspy laugh like the tail end of a kookaburra's cackle. He gets a sparkle in his eye sometimes when he's talking to me and tells jokes that are slightly off. I suspect he's had many a flirt with pretty women, but I can see that Lorna keeps him on a tight leash.

Robert is tense, perhaps because he can't tell them the real reason why we left England. His story is that he finished his work there, had the system running well, and needs a new challenge. 'I'll look for a position while we're here on holiday. I'm not going to rush into anything. I want job security and the freedom to try out new ways of using computers to connect people's research.'

His mum is very proud of him. It was she who'd encouraged him to return to study when he was a schoolteacher. I think it gratified her to have a smart kid, having given up her own career; the other two boys aren't high achievers. As for his dad, he's a small-town accountant, has given his family a secure, comfortable lifestyle, and seems quite happy with his life. He looks at Robert sometimes with a slightly puzzled expression, searching for things to say in response to Robert's monologues about computer science, quantum physics and the universe.

When the lunch dishes are washed up, I leave the girls listening to their grandma reading them stories and go into the other room to phone Mum in Sydney. I wrote to her in England and explained that we'd be living near Mackay for a couple of months while Robert looked for another position. Then we'd come down to Sydney and send some time with her before taking off to wherever it would be.

'Is everything OK?' she asks. 'I'm sure it must have been hard leaving your lovely home and all your friends.'

'Yes, Mum, we're fine. It was hard, but we had a nice little holiday at the Lakes and in London before we came back, and we've got a unit by the beach here. The two older girls will go to school while we're here and spend some time with their grandparents. They need to get to know them.'

'Ah yes,' she says. 'I'm so fortunate I had my visits with you in England.'

She'd been over twice. The first time was when Caitlin was born; she spent six months with us. It was a wonderful help for me, but having her companionship made me realise how empty my marriage was. She visited again when Penelope was a toddler. She had a few weeks with us, and then set off on the trip of her lifetime, to Greece and Crete and then to Italy. I'd asked my brothers to join with me in paying for this; I wanted her to see the sites of ancient civilisations that she'd studied all her life. She's spent her life raising five children in hard conditions of poverty and isolation, keeping the farm going after my father left us, then back to teaching when we had to leave the farm. She was very driven in her work, a dedicated teacher, and it came first when I was living with her as a student before I got married. In this, she's like Robert. She sets herself to her work and will not let anything interfere with it. She didn't retire from teaching until a couple of years ago, when she was seventy-five.

I felt upset when I was getting ready for my wedding. She always had papers to mark, and although she paid for some of my clothes and for the reception, she left all the arranging to me. When Robert's mother came to stay with us for a few days before the wedding, Mum was difficult; she was coldly polite to Lorna, and distant and critical with me. I think she was punishing me for leaving her, even though she'd pushed me into marrying Robert. I must say, though, Lorna behaved very well; she kept a low profile and did what she could in practical ways to help me with the last-minute preparations. She and Dad haven't had a chance to get to know the girls, so this time, I'll make sure they see as much of them as they can. For who knows where we'll be off to next?

The unit is very pleasant, as Dad had promised. It's two bedrooms, clean and spacious, and it's just a short walk through the dunes to the water. The girls are excited to have a new little home near the beach. Apart from a camping holiday in Spain and another at a beach in Wales, sand and ocean are new to them. Before we came out to the beach house, I went shopping with Lorna and bought them bathers and hats and she bought them some sand toys.

May in Mackay is like a pleasant English summer's day, though there's more sunshine. It's a gentle seventy-seven-degree day, with a soft breeze and a few little clouds passing over the sun now and then. So as soon as we've unpacked our things, the first thing we do is take them down to the water. Sophia and Caitlin go out in the water with Robert, up to their waists, jumping the waves, which are small and gentle, as this is a sheltered bay. Penelope and I sit near the edge of the water, making a sandcastle with a moat around it, and rebuilding it when the little waves smooth it out.

Eleven

Queensland school term two has started, and Sophia and Caitlin are enrolled at Mackay Primary School. Fortunately, the classes are mixed age groups, so they're in the same class. As for Penelope, I don't want to put her in day care – she's only two and a quarter – so I ask her grandma if she's happy to look after her while I do some classes. I have to find something to keep my mind occupied, here, amongst strangers, to fill in the time in this no-place in no-time in my life. I've found someone who teaches sketching, and I've long wanted to learn to draw again. I loved drawing and painting when I was little, but somehow, after my father left, I lost it, just as I lost my ability to imagine myself in other worlds, other dramas, and create stories of myself where I was queen or princess or witch or fairy.

We've been in the beach house for a week when Robert gets ready to go off again. He says it's to a meeting in Melbourne with some academics who want to establish a chair in computing science.

'Are you going to apply for it?' I ask as I sort the girls' school stationery and prepare their schoolbags for tomorrow, their first day at school.

'Nah, I don't think so. It's a bit early for me, as I haven't published much. I need to get a good senior research position first so I can make a name for myself in research circles. But I want to find out whether there's a prospect there in two or three years' time.'

We drive together to drop the girls at school and Penelope with her grandma. Sophia and Caitlin are a bit anxious about the new school. I've heard it's pretty traditional, not like the village school they went to in England. I turn round to remind them that they'll be in the same class and can look after each other. Penelope, in the baby seat, leans forward and reaches her arms out to me, her eyes holding a question. Perhaps she is anxious too. I take her hands and squeeze them and form a kiss with my mouth. 'Mama!' she murmurs, and settles back into the seat. This precious moment reminds me of when she was a baby, my third-born, the easiest of the three to care for. Now she is nearly two and a half, with a will of her own. She's wearing a lovely crocheted dress I had made for her before we left the farmhouse. Her eyes reflect its turquoise.

After we've dropped the girls off, we drive to the airport.

'I've left some housekeeping money in the top drawer in the kitchen,' he says as he joins the queue to check in. 'Be careful driving along that beach road. It's narrow, and some of the hoons around here drive fast.'

He kisses me on the cheek, and I stand back and watch him walk purposefully, shoulders hunched, across the tarmac. He pauses at the top of the narrow metal stairs and turns around. His free hand rises, index finger erect. His forelock lifts in a gust of wind, and he pulls his hand back, brushing the thinning ginger hair back into place. He turns and disappears through the door of the plane.

As I walk in the hot midday sun to the car, I breathe deeply. Thank god! At last I can have the bed to myself! I drive through wide streets, past stilted weatherboard houses; my heart hums, my head feels freer than it has for months.

The hour with my art teacher flies by. We drive out to a fishing village, where I sketch a yacht at anchor, using pencil, striving to catch the criss-cross of ropes and the curve of the sails. Then I drive to the grandparents' house to pick Penelope up. She has just woken from a nap, and snuggles her head on my shoulder, snuffling and murmuring.

'Mumma.' Her face is warm and moist, her eyes droopy, her petal mouth half-open.

'Thanks, Mum. Has she been good?'

'Yes, she's a good girl. She ate her morning tea and had a nice long nap.'

I carry Penelope to the toilet and squat down beside her, pulling her training pants down, and sit her on the edge of the seat, holding her while she pees.

In the hallway, my mother-in-law is waiting. She bends over to kiss Penelope's cheek. 'Bye-bye, darling. See you tomorrow.' She follows us and stands outside the screen door, shielding her eyes from the afternoon sun, waving as I back out of the driveway.

We get to the school just as the children are coming out, a swarm of little bees in bright blue trousers or skirts with sunflower yellow shirts. Sophia isn't part of the main swarm. She is with a girl she's made friends with, and they are deep in talk. Caitlin is in a group of boys and girls who are playing tag; they scatter on the playground, bags dropped and forgotten. I walk over and take Caitlin's hand, guiding her back to where her bag lies half-open, contents spilling out.

'Well, darlings,' I say as we move through the gate, 'how was school today?'

'I got all my spelling right. And I got a star.'

'Well done, darling.' I reach down and hug Sophia, feeling with a shiver of recognition her slim body, her sensitive uncertain energy.

Sophia is like I was as a little girl, unsure, shadowy in the world of adults. The kind of kid who stays in the background when adults are around, listening sometimes, more often absorbed in a world that's more real than the real world she inhabits.

'And Caitlin got in trouble,' she adds, as we walk to the car.

Caitlin now… a different story. I looked at my second daughter's untidy, solid little body, the broad face and bright blue eyes, the fuzz of red-gold curls. Where did she come from? So vibrant, so naughty.

'What happened, Caitlin? Why did you get into trouble?'

'Well…' Caitlin glares at Sophia.

'Yes?'

'Um…I were talking.'

'So what did the teacher do?'

'She maded me sit next to her desk for the rest of the lesson.'

It isn't like the village school they went to in England, where the children were allowed to move around the classroom and choose their own activities. Here, they sit behind desks in orderly rows. They are expected to be quiet and obedient, to put their hands up when they want to speak, and every class of the same grade throughout Queensland is supposed to be doing the same thing at the same time every day. Shades of Napoleon.

As I drive out of town along the red dirt road to the beach house, I wind down the window to let in some fresh air. Grey-green untidy bush frames the road, a scramble of tea trees and eucalypts and miscellaneous raggle-taggle vegetation. I recoil again from the strange smell I've never noticed in other places I've lived in. Tomcat mixed with kerosene. It took me a while to realise it isn't animal, it is the aroma of the bush in this part of the country.

Oh, for the smells of home, our English home. Even the rotting hay and cow manure on dank winter days when the cows stay in their barns. For a moment, I am back in England, driving into our laneway, past the ancient shed with its mossy rusted roof and broken timber.

The narrow dirt road that leads from the old Tudor farmhouse to the village isn't red, it is caramel colour, deepening to chocolate when it is wet, with big grey puddles reflecting the sky, and soft green grass framing the edges. A flock of geese graze along the banks of the stream. The cows have right of way when the farmer drives them to and from the meadow. If you happen to be driving and they are on their way to the rich grass beyond, you just have to sit and wait while they amble past, fat, shiny brown queens of the road. The pond in the field next to the house is shrouded in mist. The walnut tree is stark and black against winter skies, sparse of leaf in summer, as old as Shakespeare, no longer fruitful, but a favourite perch for daytime birds, and a haven for owls and other secret night-time creatures.

Lost.

*

Back in the beach house, I sit the children at the little wooden table in the kitchen and give them biscuits and juice. I send the older girls out to the veranda table to do their homework. I'll hear their reading later. I am anxious to do the next stage of my sketch and want them quiet and occupied. Penelope sits on the floor with some plastic stacking cups and rings. I get out my inks and begin to bring the tracery of lines from pale, tentative threads into a bolder life.

The phone rings in the kitchen. I take Penelope in with me and sit her on the floor next to the open kitchen drawer containing measuring cups and spoons and other innocuous items. After I put the phone down, I go back into the dining room. I see a mess. Black ink is splashed across the white page on which the yacht has begun to take sail; the bottle is overturned. A dark liquid trail oozes across the table, dripping onto white tiles. I swear under my breath. As I find cloths to soak up the ink and sponge the floor, I listen for sounds of my older children. All is quiet. I mop the excess ink on the sketch with tissues. Perhaps I can copy it and start afresh. When I've cleaned up the mess, I walk outside, holding Penelope in my arms. Sophia is sitting on the veranda, absorbed in the latest Enid Blyton book from the library, but Caitlin is nowhere to be seen.

'Sophia, do you know where Caitlin is?'

Sophia raises her eyes for a moment. She blinks, then bends her head back to the page. 'No, Mum… She went inside.'

I walk into the garden, leading Penelope, then along the path to the beach, calling Caitlin. She isn't on the beach, or in any of the usual spots where they play.

'Where Cait-ling?' Penelope asks.

'Oh, I think she's hiding somewhere. She's done a naughty thing and she doesn't want me to scold her. She'll come back when she gets hungry.'

When the sun is beginning to sink behind the fringe of bush at the back of the house, Caitlin strolls into the kitchen, nonchalant. Her flossed red-gold curls sparkle in the last shaft of sunlight falling across the room. 'Are there any bikkies left, Mum?' Her eyes are wary, scanning my face. Her hands are tucked into the pockets of her shorts.

'No. It's nearly teatime. Caitlin, show me your hands please.'

'No, Mum, I can't.'

'Why not?'

She looks at her feet and shuffles them back and forth. 'Um…it's a secret.'

'Caitlin, did you spill my ink and spoil my sketch?'

'No, Mum, I never did.' Her fists are clenched tightly in her pockets.

'Well, Penelope didn't do it because she was with me, and Sophia didn't do it because she was outside reading a book. So…don't lie to me.'

'P'raps a dog did it. I seed a big yellow dog run away.'

As Caitlin offers this story, I see again the yacht poised to sail through the rising waves, the wind plumping the sails, the ropes straining and tensing; I hear again the body of the boat creaking slightly as it moves with the swell of the water.

I pick up the spoiled sketch from the kitchen bench and show it to Caitlin. 'Look. This is what you did. I'm very cross because this was special to me.'

Caitlin looks at the sketch and drops her eyes.

'Well?'

Silence.

I look again at the black ink spread in an ugly stain across the page, mocking my painstaking work. I screw it up and toss it in the rubbish bin. 'All right.' I turn, keeping my voice quiet, resisting the impulse to punish this little girl with a will harder than mine. 'I've run a bath. You go and hop in with Sophia, and make sure you scrub your fingers. I think you've got some black ink on them, and there's a smudge on your cheek as well. I'll talk to you later about the ink.'

Caitlin runs off. Soon she and Sophia are splashing and laughing in the bath, playing their favourite characters, Princess Gloria and

Princess Marigold, the twin sisters who live in a castle in the magic forest, and have all the birds and animals of the forest as their friends and playmates.

Penelope is getting grumpy. I pick her up and sit her in her high chair with a plateful of scrambled eggs, potato and peas, her favourite meal. I sit beside her on the stool, helping her eat.

'The owl and the pussycat went to sea…two more mouthfuls, darling, and then you can have some pudding…in a beaut-iful pea-green boat…one more…with lots of honey – good girl, now pudding.'

Penelope kicks her feet happily as I serve peach jelly and custard.

'And plenty of money wrapped up in a five-pound note.'

When the last scrape of custard is gone, I pick her up and take her in to the bathroom to join her sisters in the bath. I pull off her shift and panties and lift the plump body in, sitting her between the two older girls.

Five minutes to myself. I pour a glass of Riesling. I sit out on the veranda, breathing the cool evening air, moist with sea and salt.

The phone call was from Jack, a man I met at a dinner party Robert and I went to last weekend. He is having a party soon and wants us to come. Robert will be back from Melbourne by then.

Jack's wife is a strange one. She's curvy and good-looking, with dark hair piled up and a strong face. She talks a lot and swears in every sentence. She did a line for Robert, got him talking about quantum physics, and they went for a walk together in the garden while I talked with Jack. He seemed different from the others, less small-townish. He's South African, from Johannesburg. We talked about poetry and painting, and he told me that I have an almost perfect mouth. He is an industrial designer. I wonder what a perfect mouth looks like.

What of Derek? He's a world away, he can't rescue me, he's as trapped as I am. At least he can still enjoy sex. I don't get it, how men can keep having sex with someone they don't love. For me, it's a duty that has become a bondage. It's the price I pay for having a family. As for love, I'm beginning to think it's an illusion. Romantic love has always been my dream since I was a young child. Finding a man who would love me for myself, who would share his innermost self with me. That dream shattered when Marion told us she and Derek loved each other and would stay together.

Penelope starts to cry, and I drain my glass and go in to start the next stage, drying and dressing Penelope for bed. Then story time, settling Penelope, dinner with the other two, more stories, bed for them, and then some time to myself again, time to read, to dream, to sleep. Alone.

Twelve

While Robert is away, I think a lot about my marriage. Despite his promises after the debacle with Derek, he hasn't changed. He's secretive and doesn't tell me what his plans are. I'm glad when he's away, but it's back to the old pattern. He said this would be a place for him to spend more time with us, to relax and play with the children. He takes them down to the beach and reads them stories at bedtime when he's home, but mostly during the day he goes out, plays golf with his dad and his mates, and does 'business' in town. We've been out to visit people a couple of times, friends of his parents. They are older generation, and party Queensland style, with barbecues, kids playing around the garden, a keg of beer and rum for the men, and shandies, port and lemon, sherry, or sweet white wine for the women. I can't find much to talk with them about. Their idea of travel is to go to Singapore, where the women shop and have their hair and nails done while the men play golf, and they feast on Chinese and Malaysian food.

When Robert returns from Melbourne, I ask him how his discussions about the chair in computer science went.

'Oh, good actually. It turns out they're not ready to establish the chair yet, they have to get funding for it. But they're definitely interested in considering me for it, if I can get some papers published, to show that I've forged new pathways in systems software.'

The day of the party, Robert takes the girls to his parents in the afternoon and plays nine holes of golf with his dad.

'How were the girls about staying overnight there?' I ask, as we get ready for the party.

'Excited! Mum took them to a matinee of *The Jungle Book*.'

I choose a crocheted suit, midnight blue, with a border of sea-green flowers in the sleeves and trouser legs. The top shows my midriff, and the whole thing is quite revealing because of all the holes in the pattern.

'Sexy!' he says, looking me up and down. 'I haven't seen this one before.'

When I was so unhappy, after he came back from the States and told me about the New York affair, and I was thinking of Derek all the time, I had some clothes made for me at the knitting shop in the market town near where we lived; it is a piece of England. This was the most successful of the pieces, and it's light enough to wear here. The other winter woollies are packed away in the trunk that's in storage. Along with the jumpsuit and the leather gear he gave me.

At the party, he finds an old friend he hasn't seen for years and holes up in a corner with him and a few bottles of beer. We don't dance together much, not any more. We used to enjoy jiving together. Not proper rock 'n' roll with all the moves, just freestyle. He'd move fast, bending his knees, leaning forward, fingers snapping, feet flashing, eyes sparkling. He was a bird displaying its feathers and marking its territory. His dancing with me was, I see now, a way of displaying his ownership of me and his power. Dancing wasn't a way of connecting for him; it was an exuberant expression of energy and will and lust for life, and I was caught up in the forcefield.

I dance with Jack, as close as we can get without being indecent, cheek to cheek, lower bodies held slightly apart, to the slow rhythms of Bing Crosby crooning 'Now or Never'. His energy is soft and welcoming and I feel lightly held, in tune with him.

'American Pie' comes on, slow at first. It speeds up with the chorus. He swings me round then pulls me in close as the rhythm slows again. We touch cheeks, I feel his heartbeat, then we speed up again, spun and twisted by the magic of the song.

We sink onto a soft couch as the song insists this will be the day that I die. I close my eyes, but the room is swirling.

'I've never been much good at jiving.' I open my eyes.

'You're doing all right tonight,' he says, and goes over to the bar to pour us each a rum and coke. He sits down close to me and clinks his glass against mine. 'It's not whisky and rye, but this is Queensland, not USA!'

'When I was a teenager,' I say, resting my head against the back of the couch, 'rock 'n' roll was just coming in. When I went to dances with my boyfriend, I'd wear a circular skirt with starched petticoats, tight top, bobby socks, and flat shoes. We'd bop around to "Peggy Sue" and "That'll be the Day". And when we petted in the car afterwards, I'd pretend he was Buddy Holly.'

He laughs. 'McLean wrote "American Pie" for Buddy Holly, did you know? That's what he meant about the music dying.'

'I dreamed I was Buddy Holly's bride, and when he was killed, I cried and cried.' I drain my glass.

Buddy Holly's bride was pregnant when he died. I used to think it would be so romantic having a baby with a man I loved. Him putting his hand, his face on my swollen belly, listening to the heartbeat of the child inside, feeling its little legs kick. Having him there at the birth, breathing with me, holding my hand, stroking my face as I groan and scream. Holding the little body up for me to see, placing it on my belly, stroking my cheek as I hold it, as I explore with my fingers its perfect shape.

Robert was away for each birth.

I touch Jack's hand lying next to me. His fingers close over mine. His eyes are soft, and I feel at home for the first time since I left England. Oh god, what would I give for a man I'm in tune with, feel safe with, can be myself with.

I look across at Robert. His eyes are narrowed, and his glance drops to my fingers entwined in Jack's. He lifts his beer glass to his lips, but his hand shakes, the glass shatters on the parquet floor. I uncurl my fingers. I stand up, fixed to the spot, reluctant to move away from Jack, but separate from the music, the people around me. I look over my shoulder at Jack, my eyes touching his, then turn and walk across the floor to Robert's side.

We drive home in silence. Inside, getting ready for bed, I'm wary, waiting for an outburst. He ignores me, and when we get into bed, he turns on his side, away from me, and goes to sleep. This is curious. Normally, he'd be cross-examining me.

Jack. His energy is attractive, and I enjoy talking with him. But I don't want another affair, it's too messy and difficult. He was an escape for the evening, but nothing's simple. Everything I do and say when Robert is around is noted and goes into some kind of register of my behaviour that he keeps in his head. His lack of reaction, except for that giveaway of the broken glass at the party, makes me wonder if he has a plan he's not going to tell me about.

After the party, Robert goes away again, supposedly checking out opportunities in Australian universities. Maybe he's planning to get us away from here as soon as he can.

Jack phones after he's gone and asks if he can come and see me. Caitlin and Sophia are at school, and Penelope is asleep. So, I say yes, knowing full well why he wants to see me. A voice tells me I should refuse him. But I need to talk to someone I can connect with.

I hoped, when we were in London, that with time and gentleness, Robert and I could grow closer, and I could begin to feel more loving towards him, perhaps even desire him. But here in Australia, he's retreated into the shell he has worn for years, is cut off and preoccupied, except when he's with the girls, or at night when they are asleep. Then, as before, he wants sex every night. The party night was the first time he's left me alone, apart from when he's away.

In England, I gave up hope of ever being with Derek again, and although he writes to me, addressed to my post office private box, long emotional letters in scrawled black ink with bad spelling ('I was dyslexic at school, love, so spelling is not my strong point'), I don't see the point of pretending we can be together. As before, he tells me that he fantasises about me when he makes love to Marion. I don't fantasise about him any more. Now, he's just a friend, someone I can write frankly to about how I'm feeling. I haven't really forgiven him for being so weak and cowardly and letting Marion do the talking. I thought he'd be stronger than that, given the vows of undying love he made to me.

*

It is a soft, sunny day, so Jack and I sit out on the veranda. It seems wrong to be sitting here talking to an almost-stranger who wants me, with Penelope sleeping in her cot in the bedroom off the veranda. And Robert. His shadow lies across the space between us.

We sit and talk for a while. Jack tells me of his work and a bit about his life in South Africa.

'Why did you come out to Australia?'

'I found apartheid unbearable. I protested against it actively, and I got arrested. Spent two years in prison. I was still young then. While I was in jail, I decided to leave.'

'What brought you to Australia?'

'I reckoned it would be more democratic. South Africa was a democracy in name, but only for white people. I knew that Aborigines have had a terrible history under white rule, but South Africa was ten times worse.'

He seems very open-minded and warm-hearted. I feel I could tell him anything. I tell him what a trap my marriage has become.

He says, 'I know it's harder for women, still, despite Women's Lib and all that. But Anna, my motto is, if you see something is wrong, if you're not free to live as you want to live, take your power, make a change. Even if it's too hard, if you follow your heart, you'll find a way.'

'I'd like to believe you, but right now, I can't see a way out. I can't take the children from him, and I can't leave them.'

To change the subject, I get up and make us a cup of tea. As I wait for the kettle to boil, I reflect on Jack and wonder why I've met another man who desires me, so soon after Derek.

I find it strange that he has the same profession as Derek. While we chat idly, at the back of my mind I compare the two men, the lost lover and the would-be lover. They are as different as their names. Derek is tall, Jack is small; Derek has brown hair and brown eyes, Jack has almost black hair and green eyes; Derek is fair-skinned, Jack is olive; Derek is my age, Jack is sixteen years older; Derek is dreamy, easy-going, emotional, unsure of himself; Jack is intense, talkative, and believes that you can be whatever you want to be. Worlds and a generation apart, these two men, yet they both see something in me that they desire. And they are both artists.

I move to a chair where I can see a fringe of custard-coloured sand through a break in the dunes, the teal-blue seaweedy water that meets it. The lapping wavelets and the warm, filtered sunlight still my thoughts, and make my eyes heavy. My skin softens, the knots in my neck and shoulders loosen.

Jack steps over to my chair. He strokes the back of my neck with one finger. I close my eyes.

*

When Robert returns, I tell him straight away about Jack. I want to shock him into realising it isn't going to work for us. Jack has made me realise that. Every day here, in this place, whether Robert's here or away, I've felt like a prisoner.

'Huh! Surprise me. I could see this coming a mile off,' he says, walking over to the drinks cabinet and pouring himself a whisky. 'He was all over you at the party, and I didn't see you resisting.'

He paces up and down a few times, then turns and looks at me. 'I think you should go away for a weekend with him and work out what you want to do. See how you feel about him. I'll pay your fare and expenses to go to Brisbane with him.'

I didn't expect this. It sounds as though he's worked out this plan while he was away, as though he expected this to happen. I thought he'd throw a tantrum. He doesn't seem very upset. This is so different from how he reacted in England…he must have been expecting it to happen again. Why doesn't he meet Jack and threaten him with exposure, make him back off? Jack has a business in town, he has a family, and Robert could make things very nasty for him. Not that I want him to. Maybe he doesn't want it to get out that his wife is making out with a local man. Or perhaps he doesn't care any more. This strange suggestion, that he'll pay for me to have a weekend with my lover, is a puzzle to me. Maybe he wants to use it to get rid of me.

But the children! There's no way round that. He says he can't live without them (he said that about me too, but the tune has changed) and I can't be separated from them. I'm getting into deep water here. I wish I could just say I'm leaving and taking the girls with me to Sydney to stay with my mother. That's what I should do. But he wouldn't agree to that. And I have no money of my own. He had title to the farmhouse, and the profits from the sale are in his name in a bank account.

One thing's clear. The undying love he swore in England, the promises to change, were fired by his fear of losing the children more than by his desire for me. I wonder if he is cracking up.

I accept his offer. I want to find out how I feel about Jack. Not that I can see a future with him. He's settled here in Mackay, and I couldn't live here, even if Robert and I separate. I think there's a plan behind all this, but I don't know what it is.

Thirteen

I phone Jack at his office and tell him about Robert's offer. 'Would that work for you? Can you get away for a weekend?'

'Sure, that's easy. I've got to get a contract signed with a client based in Brisbane who owns a business up here. I do want us to have some time together, so we can get to know each other better.'

'What about your wife?'

'I'll tell Marcia that I've got business appointments. But…it's a bit weird that Robert's suggested this!'

'I don't know why. I've given up trying to figure out what he'll do next. He moved us across the world to get away from Derek.' I told him about Derek that day he visited me at the beach house. We'd talked about marriage, what it's been like for each of us. Marcia is his second wife.

'So you're not happy together?'

'We were at first, but she's become an alcoholic, and has some violent rages. I've thought of splitting, but we've got three little boys, and I don't think she'd cope as a single mum. She was a fashion designer when we met, and when we started a family, she set up a home business as a seamstress. But these last couple of years, she's been drinking heavily, and her clients have fallen away. She's angry with me, thinks it's my fault. I do my best to support her and parent the kids when she's out of it, but it's hard.'

We agree on a date to fly to Brisbane. Jack will go down on Friday morning, and I'll get an afternoon plane after the girls finish school. Robert's going to take them to stay with his parents.

*

In Brisbane, we spend our two evenings and nights together talking,

talking, dining and wining, making love. Jack doesn't have the problems Derek had in expressing his desire for me. In fact, two nights is enough. I don't get much sleep. I couldn't keep this up, that's for sure! He is a good lover, but something inside me holds back. Some deep inner chamber that's locked. What is it, why do men have this need to keep entering a woman's body? It's more than a physical thing with him, and it was with Derek too. Derek said, 'It's not lust I feel for you, you know!' I didn't know what he meant then. I don't even know what lust is. My heart and my body seem to be disconnected somehow. I thought I'd opened my heart to Derek, but I know now that I didn't, because as soon as he stepped back and let Marion take over, after I'd gone through my shock and grief, I lost my feelings for him…it felt like I'd been living in a dream, then I woke up. The feelings I have for my children are the only ones I trust.

When Jack goes to his appointments in the morning, I try to shut off my mind and sleep. Then, in the afternoon, needing some fresh air, I go out and get the CityCat to New Farm Park. There, on a park bench under the giant fig trees, I sit, reflecting on this strange time in my life. I feel I'm on the cusp of change, but I don't know what form it will take. I have no one to talk to about it apart from Jack, and he has his own problems. Sounds like his wife's pretty stuck, and he's stuck with her. I haven't asked him about their sex life. Maybe he still enjoys it with her, when she's not too drunk.

I like the attention, the adoration, and I like his free thinking. Yet, he seems trapped himself. It's all very well to say, if you don't like the way your life is, change it. Perhaps it's easier for him to escape, because he has a life outside the home. And he can get away, like now, with me, and indulge his desires for love.

'You're so lovely,' he said last night when we were making love. 'You're the woman I've been searching for. Soft and affectionate, intelligent, no sharp corners. I can have a real conversation with you. And I love the fact that you don't have orgasms. I means I can go on for longer!'

I'd told him about how Robert has defined me as frigid and bought me a book on sex and a vibrator.

'Making love, for me, is getting to know someone deep down,' Jack said, resting his head on his hand and studying my face. 'Giving pleasure and receiving it comes naturally when you see someone as they are and let them see you. As for orgasms, don't worry about it. I think if you felt secure with someone who loves you, you'd let go.'

Now, in the light of day, I don't believe that I'm his ideal woman. There's no such thing. The sun is sliding behind the trees on the far bank of the lake. I watch the ducks dabbling and upending in the murky water near my seat, and wish I could live so simply, just be, without having to think about what other people think of me or want of me. Just be myself. So far, I've moved through life trying to play the roles I've been taught, dutiful daughter, student, would-be academic, wife, hostess, stay-at-home mum, hoping I'll grow into them. The only one that's felt fully real to me, part of me, part of my mind, body and soul, is being a mother. Being a lover is a part of me that's become confused with having sex with someone you don't love or having it with someone who's not yours.

That day Derek and Marion came to tell us they were going to stay together, the illusion I'd hung onto since childhood – that you can live in a world where love is the glue that holds people together, where happiness is the rule not the exception, where you can live as you please, not as others say you should – shattered.

Anyway, Jack is sixteen years older than me, he has a business in Robert's hometown, and a wife and three children. I don't want to be the cause of destroying his family. Or him to be the cause of destroying mine.

Fourteen

On Monday morning, I say goodbye to Jack at the airport and take the plane to Mackay. Robert meets me at the airport and doesn't ask me anything about the weekend. Still playing his cards close to his chest. When I met him, he was an avid poker player and met with a group of friends once a week. They'd have an all-night session, drinking and smoking and betting on their hands. He'd boast to me that he won more times than he lost.

When the girls are in bed, I ask him to sit out on the veranda with me. It is a warm autumn night.

He picks up the whisky bottle and a couple of glasses and follows me. We sit in the chairs Jack and I first sat in when he visited. Robert looks at me, sighs, and looks away. He hands me a glass and lights a cigarette.

'Robert…I'm the children's mother and your wife, but…'

He is silent.

'I'm not sure what it all means, Robert. I don't know Jack very well. And I can't leave the children.'

'So what do you want to do?' He turns his head and looks at me, frowning, his eyes narrowed.

'I don't know. I'm confused. But I know it's not working with you. I don't love you. I don't want to have sex with you any more. I'm sorry.'

Jack has at least given me this, the courage to say no. I've said it before but given in when he's pressured me. This time I mean it.

He pours himself a whisky with a shaking hand. 'You've never grown up, that's your problem. You're so insecure about yourself that you'll give yourself to any man who shows an interest.'

He gulps from his glass and stands up, turning his back to me. 'I'm well known in this town, my father's a respected professional here. I'm building an international reputation as a computer scientist. I'm building a future for my family, my children. I've given you a good life, I've taken you to places you'd never have gone to on your own. I've supported you ever since we started a family. My family means everything to me. Being a mother hasn't stopped you sleeping around. You've not only disgraced me – you've done it in my hometown. I'll be the laughing stock of the district.'

I take a deep breath and try for a way out. 'Can we stay together as parents, without being lovers?'

Robert lights a cigarette and pours himself another whisky. I look towards the ocean, listening for the sound of the waves.

'I can't live in the same house with you and see you fucking the next man who falls for you. If we're not going to be man and wife, there's only one way out.'

He wanted to see what I'd do, and now I've done what he expected. He's not stupid, he knows I don't enjoy sex with him, that I'm unhappy – he's blaming me entirely. When he had affairs, he'd come back and tell me about it, and swear he'd do nothing to break up the family. Now, with my second affair, he's labelled me an adulteress.

'So you want a divorce? What about the children?' My voice comes out wrong, not calm like I want it to be. Shrill, thin.

'You'll have to leave them with me and go and stay with your mother.' He inhales deeply and paces up and down in front of me.

I sit, stunned. I never expected he'd do this to me, to the children. I take a deep breath and try again. 'Robert…surely you don't want to deprive them of their mother?'

He passes back and forwards a few more times. 'You should've thought of them before you jumped into bed with him. I'm not giving them up.' He grinds his cigarette stub into the floor with his heel.

I want to scream, to hit him, to push him over so his head hits the rail and he never wakes up. He's set me up. I didn't expect he would do this, try to take the children from me. He knows that I'm central to their lives, that he's been an absentee father a lot of the time.

'It's you who've chosen to break up the family,' he says, with a look that deflates my murderous fantasy.

For he is right in a way. In his terms, he is right.

I hold my head in my hands and sob. 'I don't want to lose my children,' I cry. 'I've never wanted to leave them.'

He turns his back to me. 'You're not going to take them from me.'

His voice is flat, grating, like the Daleks – 'we will ex-TERM-in-ate!' I hate him.

He walks out to the back lawn and stands with his back to me, his shoulders hunched. I can hear his pee hit the grass, singeing it.

I feel the pain rising from his body. Change it, change it, it's not too late. It doesn't have to be this way.

'I don't want to take the children away from you,' I call out. 'Can't we at least live near each other? I'm willing to stay here until you find another job. You could live with your parents and see the girls every day, share in their care. Then I'll follow you with them to wherever you decide to live.'

I walk towards him as he steps back onto the veranda. I reach out to touch him, wanting to signal in some way that I care, that I don't want to hurt him any more than I already have.

He pushes past me, drains his whisky and pours another. 'What, to watch you carrying on like a whore? A fucking whore?' He resumes pacing, his gait unsteady. His voice is a stretched wire about to snap. 'Go down to Sydney and stay with your mother. We'll tell the girls that she's ill and you have to look after her.'

'But Robert...when will I see them again?'

'I have to think about my situation and decide what to do next. They can come down and visit you in the school holidays.'

'But they're so little! They need their mother!'

'They'll be fine. I'll make sure of that. Mum will help me look after them.'

'Robert, I can't leave them!'

'If you try anything, I'll kill you, kill them, kill myself – you're not going to take them from me!' he screams, and staggers down the steps and along the path to the beach.

*

While he's away, I find a spare single mattress and a blanket and pillow and put it on the floor in the girls' room. If I'm in the same room as them, he won't touch me. I lie, crying silently. They are here, but I am behind an ice wall, shut off from them. I listen to their breathing, trying to calm myself. But I can't switch off, my mind is whirling.

For the second time, I am cast as the guilty party, and he is the victim. Last time I stepped outside my fake life, he crumbled, declared his love for me and his remorse for being an absentee husband and father. I knew he'd loved other women while we were together. I found some letters from them in his desk while I was packing up our things in England. I didn't read them, but it proved what I'd suspected, that he kept in touch with them, maybe even saw them again when he was away.

Then there was the kinky sex. When we moved to England, he bought a Polaroid camera duty-free, and he used to get me to move around the bedroom and other parts of the house naked, when the children were asleep. On one of his trips, when we were living in the farmhouse, he brought back a duty-free Kodak super 8 movie camera. He said it was to film the girls while they were little, but he also used it to film me in the bath, in bed, getting dressed. The night of the knotted thongs, before I lost consciousness of what was happening, I know he had the Polaroid set to take multiple shots. He never showed me the film from that and other sessions. I imagine he used them to masturbate to. I managed to avoid a repeat of the thongs session, but I've often wondered whether he's done the same with other women. And why he wants it this way? Maybe pain with sex is a kind of opiate for him, gives him a feeling of peace? Who knows. I don't want to think about it any more.

When Derek stepped into my life that autumn afternoon, he seemed like a manifestation of the love that I had sought before I married Robert, when I was a student, a love that I dimly remembered from childhood before my father left, and I knew what it was like to be loved for no reason other than being me.

This time, after Jack, I am not the wife Robert wants to keep at all costs, I am a whore; I've proved that by doing it to him twice in quick succession. He's redefined the family, and I am no longer part of it. I need to see a lawyer, but he won't let me stay here and do that. I'm in enemy territory, I can't stay.

For the first time I am frightened of him. I can't see what to do but to agree to his terms.

Fifteen

At the airport, my girls and I sit huddled together. Penelope is curled up on my lap. Sophia is quiet and withdrawn, leaning her head on my arm.

'But Mummy,' Caitlin sobs, clinging to me tightly, 'can't I come with you?'

Sophia burrows her head into the space between my arm and my breast. Penelope wriggles and nestles in closer.

'Darling, I wish you could. But Nanna is ill, and I need to look after her for a while. I'd take you all with me if I could. But it's only for a short while, and you can come down in the school holidays.' I have to believe this myself.

Robert paces up and down a few feet away, chain-smoking, watching the clock.

We sit without words, just the sound of Caitlin's sobs and Penelope's snuffles and Sophia's sighs.

A voice announces my flight for Sydney is boarding. I hug each child wordlessly, mutter goodbye to Robert, and walk towards the departure gate. I turn before I start the long walk across the tarmac and wave, trying not to cry. They stand in a sad little cluster, Robert holding Penelope. She is crying. He has one arm around Sophia. She is clutching Bunny. On his other side, Caitlin hunches, her back to me, her face buried against her father's hip.

Orange Teddy lies on the ground, face down.

Sixteen

David, my big brother, meets me at the airport. On the drive to Hunters Hill where he and his family live, with Mum in the granny flat, I tell him a short version of the events of the last few months. I frame my own two affairs with a brief outline of what our marriage has been like since we went to England. He takes it matter-of-factly. He's been through a divorce and custody arrangements himself, and as a lawyer, sees many clients through marriage break-ups.

'Has he given you any guarantee he'll bring the girls down to see you in the school holidays? Anything in writing?' he asks as we drive over Gladesville Bridge towards Hunters Hill.

'No, he was in a very tense state of mind, I didn't want to push him any further. He threatened me with murder and suicide.'

'Hmm. Sis, try not to worry. I'll get you a lawyer. You need someone to help you get at least shared custody and a financial settlement.'

In truth, money is nothing to me. I have a few dollars. But I need to see my children, to have them with me, and they need me.

Mum is watching out her kitchen window as we pull into the driveway. She hurries out onto the lawn to greet me. 'Darling,' she says, releasing me from a hug and examining my face. 'Are you all right?'

'Oh, Mum, of course I'm not. But I'm here.'

She takes my arm and we walk together down the pathway to her flat. David follows with my suitcase. He takes it into the spare room, then comes out and gives me a reassuring hug.

'Chin up, sis. We'll see you through this. I'll leave you to tell the story to Mum. We'll see you both at dinner tonight, six o'clock.'

Over a cup of tea, I go over the events that led to my flight, and his reaction when I returned from Brisbane. I spare Mum all the details I can, but I'm honest about my inability to tolerate Robert's sexual demands and the emptiness of my marriage apart from my children.

Mum thought the sun shone out of Robert when we got married. For her, he was the model of a hard-working, intelligent, ambitious man, who was steady and reliable and knew where he was going. They understood each other, for they both value reason and knowledge, although he is a scientist and she is a humanist and classics scholar. She never actually asked about how I felt about him. She had, in a way, chosen him for me, after seeing enough of him to think that he would be a good husband and father. She'd confronted him about his 'intentions' and let him know in no uncertain terms that she expected him to marry me.

So it's hard for her to accept that he is not the perfect match she thought he was. She doesn't say much about my two affairs, but I can see she is thinking that no matter what he did when away from home, I was wrong to take lovers.

She is a curious mix of a pioneering warrior and a traditional housewife. She kept the farm going when my father left, learning to drive at the age of fifty-two, taking on all the outside work that she'd never done, getting men in to do the harder tasks she didn't have the strength or the skill for, negotiating in a man's world of station managers, bankers, stock and station agents, all those men who controlled property and money and legal arrangements in the outback. Yet, despite my father's abjection and desertion of the family and the ultimate betrayal of his return to dispossess her and sell the farm, she still believes that the man is the head of the house and the woman is the keeper of the domestic hearth and nurturer of husband and children.

This is my legacy, this divided identity. My mother was the dominant influence in my childhood, in her continuing presence and commitment to me and to her other children. But my father shadowed my childhood in his absence, and I spent my youth mourning for that lost love and longing to find a replacement, even after I had killed him off in my heart, for his failure to keep in touch with me, to let me know he loved me and I was not the cause of his leaving.

There's a chink in Mum's armour now. The man she thought would carry me with him in his career has turned into a man who will threaten murder and suicide to keep his little daughters with him, away from their mother. A conundrum. For much as she believes that the man is head of the household, in her own life she triumphantly lived the principle that the mother's role is to bring up her children, to see to their education, to give them the best start in life that she can no matter how hard the circumstances are. But then, my father was not Robert. He may have been inadequate, unreliable, manipulative and cowardly, but he was not cruel and ruthless. I think now, looking back on his failure to keep in touch with me after he left, that he was ashamed and felt he was not worthy to be my father.

When five o'clock comes, Mum, true to form, prepares Sao biscuits with cheddar cheese and pours us each a dry sherry. This is her evening ritual. We sit in her pleasant lounge room, looking out the French windows at her strip of garden. The large port-wine magnolia that she got David to plant for her when they first moved in here is covered in spear-shaped buds, blushing magenta.

'Your port-wine magnolia has grown into a stately tree, Mum,' I say, wanting to steer the conversation away from painful topics.

'Yes, it will be lovely in a month or two, when the buds open. It's my winter glory.' She clears her throat. 'Anna, what's happening with the girls? Who's looking after them?'

'Robert's mother is. He's moved in with them.'

'How do the girls get on with their grandparents?'

'Oh, good. She's kind and calm with them. She's been seeing quite a lot of them in the month we've been there. She looked after Penelope when I was doing my sketching lessons. And they love their grandad. He's funny and affectionate and spoils them.'

'Do his parents know why you've come down here?' She drains her sherry glass and looks at mine, which is empty. 'A little more sherry?'

'Thanks, Mum. I'm sure he's told them by now. He didn't tell them before I left this morning. At least he spared me that. They thought I was coming down because you were ill. That's what we told the girls too.'

'I'm so worried about them, each of them! Especially Penelope. How old is she now?'

'She'll be two and a half in July. So she's only twenty-eight months old!' I feel a lump rising in my throat. 'I'll be back in a minute.'

In the bathroom, I close the door, sit on the toilet, and let the sobs I've been holding back since I left rise up. My chest's been feeling as though it's locked in a vice, and it hurts to breathe. After a few minutes, I go to the basin and wash my face, then go out to Mum again.

She looks at my face and gets up to clear away the glasses and plates. 'Well, darling, what's done is done. Let's hope that he'll see reason and come down to talk things over with you.'

The family dinner with David and his wife, Jo, is easier than being alone with Mum. Jo gives me a warm hug and her eyes shine with fellow feeling. She went through the separation from her husband, when David and she fell in love, and the shared parenting arrangements were thrashed out between them…a compromise, but the best that could be managed. At least the two sets of parents were able to talk to each other like adults and put the children's best interests first. And they all live in the same suburb. David's legal experience probably gave him an edge in the negotiations, and it was all made easier because, after he and Jo got together, their partners decided that they too were meant for each other. David told us that Jo is the love of his life.

So it was a wife swap between neighbours and friends, and hit the middle pages of the *Sunday Sun*, much to Mum's humiliation. But David's confidence and suave good humour are the mask for a strong will and sense of entitlement to be who he wants to be and do what he thinks best. He was the firstborn, thirteen years older than me, and he's always been Mum's golden boy. She'd forgive him anything.

While David and Mum are talking, I follow Jo into the kitchen.

'Anna,' she says, as she takes the roast out of the oven and makes the gravy, 'this must be incredibly hard for you. You know you can come and talk to me about it any time you need to. How were the girls when you left?'

'Oh, Jo, it was heart-breaking. They clung to me and cried. We've never been separated for more than a few hours before. I've always been there for them. But they think I'm here to look after Mum, and they'll be coming down to join me in the school holidays.'

'Has Robert agreed to that?' She tastes the gravy and adds another splash of wine to it.

'He did say, at the airport, that he'll let them come and visit me then. But there's no guarantee he will.'

'Bastard! How can he do this to them! What kind of a man will force a mother to leave her own children when they're so little? Or at any time?'

I have no answer. I thought I knew Robert well, but I never thought he would do this. How naive I've been.

I ask Jo about how they got together, searching for some light on the mysteries of love and desire and betrayal.

'Oh, it was a *coup de foudre*. Like being hit by lightning. I knew nothing would ever be the same again.'

'Have you ever regretted it?'

'Yes, often, every time I send my kids off to their other family or see how it has affected them. If I had my time over, I wouldn't do it. It wasn't that my first husband and I didn't get on. I'd simply grown up. When we first got together, I thought he was god. Now, sometimes, I think I've married the same bloody man!'

She laughs and lights a cigarette. It's her bad habit, she says. David wants her to give it up, but she says she needs it. She has an elegant way of holding the cigarette and inhaling lightly, pausing to watch the trail of smoke, contemplating her thoughts. Her wisdom is subtle, and she has a quiet way of observing others and thinking before she speaks.

At the dinner table, David pours me a glass of red wine. 'Try this one, Sis. It's from our latest wine bottling. It's a full-bodied red from the Barossa.'

'How often do you have bottlings?'

'As often as we need to! We've got a group of friends who share the cost of buying the cask, and we get together in the garage and do the bottling and corking, then taste the fruits and have a buffet meal. It's great fun, and much cheaper than buying retail!'

'Yes,' Mum says, 'I'm lucky. He keeps me supplied with Riesling.'

Mum has a couple of glasses of wine with dinner every night, as well as the five o'clock sherry. When we lived on the farm, I don't think she ever drank until after Dad left. When the seasons improved and the wool prices went up, she'd buy a case of Sauternes and sip a glass or two after dinner. If she weren't so disciplined, she'd be a heavy drinker. I drink more than I should now. I've always been able to drink a lot at parties, but it was only in the last couple of years of my marriage that I started drinking wine every day.

After dinner, we sit in the lounge room for a while, and while Jo and Mum are discussing Mum's recipe for lemon meringue pie, which is legendary in the family, David sits next to me.

'Anna, I've lined up a lawyer for you. Danny Chalmers. He can see you tomorrow. Get the ferry into town. You need to be at his office in Macquarie Street at three p.m. He's a friend of mine, a lovely bloke. He'll help you to get a sensible conversation going with Robert about a separation settlement and custody. It's vital to start the process as soon as possible. From Robert's form so far, I wouldn't trust him a mile off. We need to get you and the girls some safeguards.'

I go to bed feeling a little less embattled. David's and Jo's support and Mum's loyalty, even though I know she judges me for my affairs, help me to feel less alone.

*

On the ferry on my way into the city to see Danny, I allow myself to imagine how it might have been. It could have stayed the same, my world, if I hadn't taken that next step after the party. If I hadn't accepted Jack's advances, if I hadn't given Robert the chance to set me up as an adulteress, if I hadn't let him force me into leaving the girls with him. How could I let him do that? How could I let him make me the deserter, when he's been away from home more than he's been with his family all these years?

I stand at the stern, watching the whitewater froth and churn; my eyes rest on the edges of the wake, curling over to meet the swell of the harbour, roughened in the fresh breeze.

Maybe it isn't too late to mend things. If I could get him to take me back, I'd be with the children. I might be able to return to study, to get that higher degree in English literature that I abandoned to have Sophia. Maybe he'd find himself a lover again and take the pressure off me to respond to him sexually.

As the ferry chugs into the quay, I make my way to the gangway through the smell of diesel and the throb of the engines. As a child, I always daydreamed, escaped without leaving. Perhaps Robert is right. I've never grown up.

I walk up the steep hill from the quay towards Macquarie Street through the crowd of shoppers and office workers.

Robert. I am not with him any more, but he still rules my life. I am still trapped. It is just a worse kind of trap. I've lost the only beings I've ever loved without question, without reserve. And I've robbed them of the trust and security that every child should have. I can't bear to think about the effect it is having on them.

I walk into the lawyer's chambers and give my name to the receptionist.

No one can help me. I have dug myself into a pit I cannot climb out of. And Robert has watched me do it. He even helped me dig deeper and threw dirt in on top of me.

In the office on the seventeenth floor of a building that towers above Macquarie Street, after a long wait, I sit opposite Danny. He's older than me, with curly dark, greying hair and warm brown eyes. He asks his secretary to bring us coffee and offers me a cigarette. I answer his questions, telling him of my two affairs, the pattern of our marriage, with Robert at work long hours and often away at conferences, the two affairs he's had that he told me of, and his threats of murder and suicide if I tried to take the girls from him. I feel I can tell him anything and he won't be shocked or judgemental. His attention never strays from my face, except to jot down notes.

After a couple of hours, punctuated by several cups of coffee and two or three cigarettes, he leans back in his chair and closes the folder of notes. 'Anna, you don't have a problem! There are things we can do. Don't give yourself such a hard time. I'm not saying the way you went about it was wise. But under pressure, we all do things we regret. You did it the only way you could at the time. What we have to do now is find a way for you to see your children and look at whether it's possible to get custody of them, or at least joint custody. Nothing's forever, Anna. Things change, sometimes in ways you don't expect.'

I leave Danny's office feeling less desperate. His voice stays with me, and I can still hear it – the warmth, the authority, the understanding. My mind returns to times I'd forgotten, times when I was alone but didn't feel lonely, when garden, river, plains and sky encircled me, when my mother and father were together, and I felt loved.

I go back to Hunter's Hill with some hope in my heart. When I get home, I phone Robert's parents' number.

Lorna answers the phone. In answer to my question, 'How are the girls?' she replies coldly,

'They're fine. Do you want to speak to them?

'Yes, please.'

Sophia and Caitlin tell me about their day at school and ask how Nanna is.

'We miss you, Mummy! When are you coming back?' says Sophia.

'Darling, I need to stay here for a while. But Daddy has promised to bring you down to stay with me in the school holidays. That's less than a month away!'

I go through the same question and answer with Caitlin.

And when I speak to Penelope, she says, 'Mumma, when...?' Her voice trembles, and I imagine her soft face twisted and her grey-green eyes welling with tears. Oh, to hold her again.

'Darling, Daddy will bring you to see me and Nanna soon. I love you to the skies and back.'

Then I ask to speak to their grandmother again. She sends them to the living room to watch cartoons, and I ask her how they are, really. It's awkward, as I know she doesn't want to talk to me, but I need to know how they are coping. To her credit, she gives me a report of their day, how they are sleeping, what they are eating, what she and Dad have planned for them at the weekend. I ask her if Robert's away again, and she says yes, he's gone to Brisbane and will be back by Monday. Maybe he's gone to see a lawyer.

Next day, there's a letter from Jack. He's full of concern for me and wishes he could be with me to support me.

> If you get a place of your own, I want to come down and visit you. Wherever you are. I don't want to lose touch with you. Remember, just keep believing in yourself, and things will work out. I don't believe Robert will keep the children away from you. I'm sending you positive thoughts.

I don't feel anything when I read these words. What does he know about Robert and what he's capable of? He has no power to help me. He means well, but his business and his family are his life, and I'm not part of it. Apart from my family here, I'm on my own.

Seventeen

A week has passed since I left the girls. I've written to them and sent them a tape with songs and stories I've recorded. And I've spoken to their grandmother again. She says that Penelope has started waking during the night. When Robert's there, he takes her into bed with him. When he's not, she sends Grandad in to her. He picks her up and sings to her in his raspy voice until she falls asleep again. Sophia and Caitlin are doing OK, she says, though Caitlin has had a detention at school for playing up during class.

Late at night, when Mum is in bed and I'm sitting up reading, trying to keep the fears and worries out of my head, Robert phones me. He's in Sydney again and wants to meet. In the morning, I ask Mum if he can come to dinner here. I think it will be easier to have her there when we talk.

'Of course,' she says. 'I'll do his favourite, roast lamb.'

'But…how do you feel about him visiting, Mum? After all, he forced me to leave the children, and he's not made any commitment yet to discussing shared custody.'

'Well, I'm sure there were faults and mistakes on both sides. I don't want to defend him. But I'd like to hear what he has to say.'

'But Mum, you know what it was like for you when Dad abandoned his family. Now, Robert's making out that I'm doing the same thing. But there's a huge difference. Dad left for whatever reasons, and he made no effort to keep in touch with us children or to honour his promise to you about signing over the property. I left Robert because he threatened me with murder and suicide. I didn't leave my children of my own accord. He forced me to.'

Mum looks at me, lost for words for once. Then she sighs and closes the book she's been reading. 'Well, as you say, dear, they are very different stories. But he's the father of his children, and I think it's important to keep the bridge between you open as much as possible.'

*

Robert sits opposite me, eating Mum's dinner, washed down by plenty of David's home-bottled red. He is here, he says, to discuss 'the situation'. His appetite is good, as always. By the time he's finished with his plate, wiping his bread round it to soak up the gravy, it looks as though it hasn't been used. I took a small helping, but I can't finish it. I've had no appetite since I left the girls.

Robert and Mum are discussing politics as usual.

'So,' Robert says, draining the last drops of wine in his glass, 'it looks like we're getting out of Vietnam at last.'

'Yes, indeed,' says Mum, taking his empty plate, 'And not before time! Such a waste of lives, ten long years.'

'Billy McMahon's showing some sense for once.'

Robert knows that Mum's a died-in-the-wool Liberal voter, while he's a swinging voter – 'I use my reason to vote with, not my prejudices!' – but he likes to get a rise out of Mum.

Their voices rise and fall. I stare at an old stain in Mum's embroidered tablecloth. I wish this night would end soon. They're talking as if the world isn't falling apart, as if I'm not in danger of losing my children forever, as if none of what's happened in this mess of a marriage of mine that Mum so much wanted for me is of any importance. Then again, I don't want them to talk about the marriage and its ending either. I suspect they'd find some common ground, as they usually do. So politics serves to conceal the elephant in the room.

Robert asks Mum if she has any brandy, and she gets her bottle of Hennessy's out of the cupboard. She keeps it for cooking.

He pours himself a generous measure and clears his throat. He takes a sip and looks at me. 'Here, this is to help you get yourself set up in a flat. What are your plans for supporting yourself?' He pulls out his wallet and hands me a cheque. It's for a thousand dollars.

'Thank you, Robert. I'll need to get some training, since I haven't worked for eight years. I'll have to get work straight away, probably as a waitress. I did that when I was a student. My best option in the long run is to do a higher degree so I can get a uni job.'

'Well, it's up to you. I'll need all the money that's left to set up a home for the girls and see to their education and health expenses.'

Mum stands up to clear the dishes from the table. I rise to help her, but Robert waves his hand at me.

'Sit down a minute. I've something more to say.' He clears his throat and fixes his eyes on me. 'I've been offered a job in America. It's a great opportunity. I've looked into job prospects here and there's nothing to compare.'

'But…what about the children?'

'Naturally, I'll take them with me. We've already agreed their home is with me.'

'I didn't agree to that. You threatened me with murder and suicide and forced me to leave, remember? I can't agree to you taking them to America. How often will we be able to see each other?'

'You should have thought about all this before you jumped into bed with Jack, and –'

'What?' I interrupt. 'Remember you suggested I spend the weekend with him and paid my return fare to Brisbane? What was that about?'

Mum's eyes widen. I hadn't told her this detail, just that I'd been to Brisbane with Jack. I don't want to stir him up, but I'm not going to let him get away with this distorted version of what happened.

'You know how important my career is – it's not just for me,' he says, ignoring my question and draining his glass. 'I want my children to have the best prospects life can offer.'

'What sort of prospect is it to grow up without their mother?'

'This is your choice. You sign a form saying you agree to me taking the girls with me to the States, and I'll guarantee you access at least once a year.'

His eyes are Arctic blue. His lower lip is sucked in to form a tight line, showing his small, regular upper teeth. I know this look well. He empties his glass and reaches for the bottle.

Mum has said little so far. She walks back to the table on the pretext of clearing the last dishes and turns to me with a nod. 'Robert's right, Anna. You should've thought of the consequences before you left. He's made an offer. Maybe you should consider it.'

I jump up from the table and start to walk away, then turn around to face her. She gazes at me, her hands full of dishes.

'How dare you! How dare you judge me! You have no idea what this marriage has been like for me!'

Mum glares back at me. For a moment, I am a little girl again, defying my mother's authority. I take a step back towards the table. Robert's lips are puckered, ready to sip from the cut crystal glass. The golden liquid tilts towards its rim. His throat stretches up to it.

'And you, you bastard, sitting there getting drunk on Mum's brandy, eating her food…why don't you get out of here?'

Robert doesn't seem surprised. He takes a big swig, rearranges his lips, and looks up at my mother with a knowing smile. 'Well, Mrs Anderson, you see what I've had to struggle with. I've tried to talk reason to her but I'm afraid your daughter is not making sense. It's impossible to have a rational discussion with her.'

'Get out! Get out, you fucking bastard!'

I throw my shoe at him. I miss. His brandy glass smashes, spilling the last of the golden liquid on Mum's embroidered tablecloth.

Eighteen

Mum and I don't speak to each other in the morning. When I get up, she's reading the paper, and it's as if I'm not here. I guess she thinks I've behaved badly again, losing my temper, challenging her authority.

I phone Danny and briefly tell him of Robert's ultimatum, and he offers to act as mediator. I phone Robert and, to my surprise, he agrees to meet me at Danny's office.

I wait for him downstairs in the foyer. He arrives looking tense.

'Robert, before we go up, let me say, I'm sorry for losing my temper last night. I got such a shock when you said you're going to take them to America. Last time we spoke, you said you'd look for a position in an Australian university.'

His eyes are sharp and cold, his mouth tucked into a straight line. 'I'm afraid that's not possible. Let's see this lawyer chap of yours.'

Danny is waiting for us. He is relaxed and friendly, but respectful. 'Well, Dr Anderson, Anna has told me some of the history of this situation. I'm not here to judge or to mediate your relationship. My concern is for the children, for their happiness and security. I understand you plan to take a position in America and to take them with you. Before any bridges are crossed, can we pause for a moment? Can we look at how we can help them to keep their bond with both of you and grow up with access to both their parents, even if you're living apart?'

Robert softens a little. 'My girls mean the world to me.' His voice cracks, and he takes a gulp of water. 'I've been away a lot, building my career, but this break-up has made me realise how much I've sacrificed, and I want to make up for that. I want to give them the best opportunities in life, and I want them to know I'm always there for them.'

'I appreciate that,' says Danny. 'I know how hard it is to make time for family life. Before we know it, our kids have grown up. But now, while they're little, they need to see both parents as often as possible, and know they are loved by both.'

Robert glances at me. 'Anna has been a good mother. But it was her choice to break up the family. I'd have done anything to keep the family together.'

Anything as long as you could have your own way, pursue your career, have your affairs on the side when you travel. And it's your choice to break up the family, not mine.

I look up and meet Danny's eyes.

'What has happened has happened,' Danny says, 'and we need to find the best way forward. Your children are very young. How old is the youngest?'

'Penelope was two in January, so she's not yet two and a half,' I say, glancing at Robert. 'She's not even fully toilet-trained. I only stopped breastfeeding her when she was fifteen months old, before we left England. Caitlin has just turned five, and Sophia's seven.'

Robert's eyes are fixed on the floor.

After more toing and froing, and some gentle comments from Danny about the importance of having both parents when children are little, Robert relaxes a little.

'All right. I'll bring them down to visit you for two weeks in the school holidays. And we'll talk some more then about access arrangements.'

Danny leans forward. 'May I make a suggestion?'

Robert nods.

'It would be good if you can find a lawyer in Sydney so that you have a legal representative in the discussions. These are difficult and sensitive matters and having a third party present for each of you is the best way to handle it.'

'Yes, I've contacted a bloke who was recommended to me in Brisbane.'

I wait for Danny to reply. I'm struggling to stay calm. I want him to lead the dialogue, for I know that when Robert and I talk about things like this, it can go haywire very quickly.

'Dr Anderson, I know you have your children's interests at heart, and I'm sure you appreciate they need to see their mother as much as possible. What are your thoughts about Anna's access to the girls if you go to America?'

'Well, I want her to have as liberal access as possible. I'm thinking of a three-month visit the first year, and at least a month a year after that.'

I hunch my shoulders. One month a year! Eleven months of the year living thousands of miles away from them. I stare at the floor, trying not to cry. It's hopeless. He has possession of the children, money, qualifications for a well-paid job, plenty of connections – and all I have is my relationship with my girls, which he has broken. I won't let it stay broken. I'll do whatever I have to do to get access to them.

Danny looks down at his desk, closes his eyes for a minute, then looks at Robert and at me. 'I realise that you have some big decisions to make. I'm confident that you'll make your decision carefully, with the girls' needs for their mother in mind. I suggest both you and Anna take time to think carefully about this. And as soon as you've found a lawyer, preferably while you're in Sydney on this visit, we need to get together again and try to reach an agreement that puts the children's interests at the heart of things.'

I think Danny's realised that trying to discuss access now is not going anywhere, since Robert has all the cards and is keeping them close to his chest. I imagine that his strategy is to wait till Robert has his own lawyer, so he feels less threatened, and then he might be able to shift things, to get some concessions by pleading the best interests of the children.

Robert's face is closed now. I suspect he's already made his mind up and is just going through the motions here. He stands up and thanks Danny and says he'll be in touch.

'I'll see Robert out, Danny,' I say, implying that I'll come back up to debrief with him.

Together we walk out of Danny's office and down to the street. It's a grey and windy day; we stand in the shelter of the foyer. I decide to dive down beneath the fear and doubt and suspicion, and reach out to him, appeal to his love for the children.

'Robert – I'm sorry for all that's happened. I'm sorry for hurting you. I hope we can work something out so that we can both be the best parents we can be for our girls. That's all that matters now. We've given them such a lovely start in life, it would be a tragedy for them to feel they've lost me.' I'm trying to phrase it so that he doesn't feel I'm saying I'm more important to them than he is. But I know that I am. They're used to him not being around much, but I've always been there for them, till now.

To my surprise, his face softens. He puts down his briefcase and holds out his arms. I echo his gesture, and we stand close, our bodies remembering the times of happiness and shared experience. Here, in this grey official place in this windy city, for an instant, it seems possible to dissolve hurt, distrust and bitterness, and take a different path forward.

'Well…I must go. I'll see a lawyer while I'm down here, and we'll meet again, talk some more.' Robert drops his arms, kisses me on the cheek and picks up his briefcase.

I watch him walk out of the building, then go back to see Danny for a debriefing.

He leans back in his chair and gazes out the window for a few moments. 'Anna, I didn't raise the issue of a financial settlement with him today. That would have put his back up even more. I always look at the glass half full, but my experience in family law tells me we always need a plan B. I think your husband is a very intelligent man. He's also calculating. He's already shown that he's capable of making plans that will leave you stranded with no power in the situation and put you in the wrong. He may be afraid you'll apply for custody, now you know he's planning to take them out of the country. It would interfere with his career plans, that's for sure. He wouldn't be able to leave the country till it's settled. That's why he wants your agreement. Once he takes the children out of the country, you'd have little hope of getting custody if you decided to go for it. You'd have to contest it in the American court system, which would be expensive, and if he's set up there, with possession as a parent, a home and a good job, he'll have a big advantage. He'll have to make a decision soon, if it's true he's been made an offer by an American university. Do you think we should allow for him doing something rash, and take out a restraining order to stop him taking the children out of the country without your consent?'

'I think that would put his back up even more. He feels I've wronged him and humiliated him. If I put a legal hold on him, he'll try and find some more devious way of keeping the children away from me. I just don't know what he's capable of.'

'For now, at least while he's showing he's willing to negotiate, I agree, we should move softly but firmly. We need to get a formal agreement as soon as possible. And some money for you, so you can start your life again as a single woman.'

'The farmhouse in England was in his name, and the profits from the sale went into his bank account. I haven't worked, apart from some online coding for him, and he claimed for that from his workplace, since we had our first child. In any case, I don't want much. Just enough to help me get some professional training so I can get a decent job. If he keeps the children, he'll say he needs it all to provide a home for them. He's already told me that.'

'Nevertheless, Anna, since you've been the main carer of the children, you are entitled to a share. How much would be determined by the court, looking at his assets and liabilities and your contribution to the family life. There ought to be a proper settlement.'

'Danny, the money's less important to me than having my children with me. I can't think about anything else just now.'

'Of course, and I'll do my best to help you with that. But it's part of the process. If you need to get some training to get a decent job, how much do you think it will cost?'

'Oh, I don't know. The only thing I can think of is doing a higher degree so I can get an academic teaching job. I might be able to get a scholarship again to pay the fees, on the strength of my first degree. But I'd still need to live. Whatever it would cost me to pay rent, eat, et cetera. I'll make enquiries about the degree scholarship and try and work out what I'd need to live on.'

'In the meantime, what will you do to make ends meet?'

'I've found a waitressing job in Balmain. He gave me a cheque for a thousand dollars last night, to set up in a flat. He implied that's all I'll be getting. I'll start looking for one.'

Danny settles back in his chair and gazes out at the distant foothills of the Blue Mountains, veiled by a yellow-grey haze over the western suburbs. He closes his eyes for a moment and seems deep in thought. He opens them and smiles at me.

'A lot depends on what sort of bloke he chooses as his lawyer, Anna. If he gets one who has the children's interests at heart, there's a good chance we can find a compromise so that you can get on with your lives separately and share what you have in common. He's got all the cards, but if we can appeal to his good nature rather than his fear…'

Nineteen

Sophia and Caitlin want to ride on the merry-go-round. They climb onto brightly painted ponies with long manes and tails that swing out as they sweep round on movable poles. I want to sit with Penelope in a little carriage on the fixed platform, but they are all full, so I hold her in front of me with the pole between us on one of the bigger ponies. The music starts, we begin to move. We are going faster and faster, the ponies swing out higher and higher. The faces in the crowd become blurred. The centrifugal force of the racing ponies is so strong I can barely hold on to Penelope. I cling to her, my arms aching. I can feel her body being pulled away from me. I open my mouth to scream to call for help for the merry-go-round to stop but no sound comes out. I can hold on no longer – Penelope flies from my arms up into the air across the heads of the crowd.

I wake, struggling for breath, wondering where I am. I hear the roar of traffic in Darling Street, three storeys down, and smell the harbour breeze coming through the window. I'm in the little one-bedroom flat I found on the border of Birchgrove and Balmain. On the wall above my bed is Caitlin's painting of flowers in reds and purples that her grandma sent me, along with other drawings and scribbles done by the three of them. It will soon be school holidays and the girls will be with me.

I haven't heard anything more about Robert's plans since he said he'd get a lawyer in Sydney so we can negotiate. I've written to him, but he hasn't answered, except for sending me a note that I can have the old Vauxhall station wagon; he said it was parked outside the Physics department at Sydney Uni. So he must have driven it down and decided to leave it for me. He enclosed the keys, but I don't have the rego papers.

The phone is ringing. I struggle up from my bed and run into the living room. 'Hello?' My voice is choked by the scream I couldn't utter in my dream. I listen to the voice at the other end of the phone.

'Anna, I'm ringing to tell you I'm in Los Angeles, on the way to Boulder, Colorado. I've got a position at the university there.'

His voice is thin and harsh; I can hardly hear him. The line is crackling.

My mouth opens to speak, but my tongue is thick, paralysed. My throat closes.

'The girls are with me. They're fine.'

A hoarse rattle pushes up from my chest. 'But Robert…I didn't… you said…'

'You're a deserting wife and abandoning mother and you'll never see them again!'

The phone clicks. I sink down onto a chair and stare out at the water glinting in the morning sunlight beyond the rooftops.

*

I'm not sure how long I've been sitting here. What time was that phone call? I look at the clock. It's one p.m. Must have been a couple of hours ago. I stand up and gaze around me. Must do something. I'll try and phone Danny. He said to let him know if I hear from Robert. I pick up the phone and dial his work number, but the receptionist says he's out. I leave a message.

I won't ring Mum yet. I need to collect myself. She'll be very shocked, and I don't feel strong enough to tell her. So I dial Jo's number, hoping she'll be home.

'Hello? Jo, it's Anna.' I take some deep breaths.

'Anna, you sound upset. What is it, dear?'

'I've had a phone call from Robert. He's in Los Angeles. He says he's taken the girls to America. He says I'll never see them again.'

I hear her voice, but her words aren't sinking in.

'Anna, are you there?'

'Yes, sorry.'

'You must be in shock. I'll come over. I'll be there in half an hour.'

Some time later, could be minutes or hours, there's a knock on the door. I walk stiffly over. It's Jo. She holds out her arms. My tears spring onto her chest.

She leads me over to the table and sits me down, and pulls the other chair close to mine. 'My dear, this is such a shock for you. Did you have any inkling this might happen?'

'Well, he did say, that night he came to Mum's for dinner, that he was going to take a position at an American university. When we met after that in Danny's office, he said he'd get a lawyer and we'd talk about access. He hasn't said any more about it since then. He was supposed to be coming down with the girls in two weeks' time, and we were going to meet with our lawyers and discuss the next step.'

Jo persuades me to get dressed. When I emerge, she's made a pot of coffee and some toast. 'Sit down, and have some coffee and a bite to eat, if you can.'

We sit in silence for a while.

'Have you spoken to Danny yet?' she asks, pouring the rest of the coffee into my mug.

'No, he's out. I've left a message.'

'I think you should come home with me. Have dinner with us and stay overnight. I don't want you to be on your own tonight.'

On automatic, I find my nightie and toiletries and put them in an overnight bag. She leads me down the stairs to her car.

I don't care where we go. I am nowhere. I can see no future and I've lost the past.

*

Two days later, I wake from a troubled sleep. I'm back in my flat, and the clock says it's ten a.m. Jo drove me home late yesterday and gave me some tranquillisers –'Take one before you go to bed, and you can take another if you wake up and can't go back to sleep.'

After I've had a pee and washed my face, I drink a couple of glasses of water, then make a coffee. I try to phone Danny, but his secretary says he's with a client. He'll call me back.

What to do? I try to unscramble my thoughts and scribble some notes on a piece of paper. I should write to Robert. I don't even know his address, but I know he is on his way to the University of Colorado, so I suppose I can address it to him there. I need to speak to Danny first. What can I say to Robert? Whatever I say, it won't make any difference now.

At last, the phone rings. I make an appointment to see Danny this afternoon.

*

When I sit down opposite him, I can't find any words. I start to cry, and he walks around and puts his arm around me. I lean into him and cover my face. I take a deep breath and straighten up, blow my nose.

Over coffee and a cigarette, he advises me to write to Robert, just a short letter, reiterating that I need access to the children, appealing to his better nature.

'No doubt he'll get a lawyer over there. We'll need to find you an American lawyer to represent you.'

'Danny, I have no money! I don't know how I'll pay for that.'

That came out wrong. It sounds as if I'm asking for charity. Already, Danny is doing his work for me for nothing. When I protest, he says that twenty-five per cent of his work is pro bono, and that it is the least he can do.

'Anna, don't worry about that. I'll find you someone and see what his fees will be. We'll work it out. If we can work with Robert's better instincts, it may not be too complicated a process, and not too costly. I think, now he's done this, he may be less fearful, and if he's not acting out of fear, he may be more inclined to meet us halfway.'

'I think I should have put a restraining order on him. But I didn't think he would really do this. I thought he would reconsider after that meeting we had with him.'

'I did wonder, when I had a letter from the bloke he got to represent him here. I don't know him personally, but I've heard he takes a hard line.'

'He's so devious, I'm beginning to realise he's been planning this for months. He even persuaded me to let the children have their own passports before we left England. He said it wasn't fair they should be on mine.'

'Well, he had all the cards, didn't he? The money, his career, back in his hometown in Australia, his family nearby, your family far away. He had you in a very weak position.'

'I think he expected I would try to escape from him. That affair I had when we were staying near his family…'

'Yes, it does seem he set a trap for you. You not only gave him an excuse for throwing you out, but gave him evidence of your infidelity. Though it would sound fishy in court, if we revealed that he suggested it and paid your expenses! Maybe another reason why he jumped the gun and left the country with them.'

'Yes, maybe you're right. It is hard to get inside his head. What he's done is outrageous, I find it hard to believe it's really happening.'

*

At home on my own again, I open a bottle of David's home-bottled wine and sit out on the balcony, watching the lights across Iron Cove towards Drummoyne. The glassy black of the harbour sparkles and dances with lights of moored ships and factories on the shores of Drummoyne. Large red letters, DUNLOP, reflected as spilt scarlet flame on black satin, are a landmark by which I navigate as I let my consciousness float and bob on the water's oily surface. There is no wind; the only sounds are the dull hum of traffic across Iron Cove Bridge and the occasional squeal of tyres in a nearby street as some night reveller blunders home. The dying light of the old moon is reflected from the roofs of office buildings, factories, flats and tenement houses. I seem to be the only one in the neighbourhood awake, apart from a stray black cat that prowls across the rooftops and drops down into the weed-choked backyard of the next-door delicatessen, looking for the small rodents that work the night shift.

I am the night watcher on the balcony, waiting for the dawn, for it to be light, so that my demons can sleep and I can return to unconsciousness for a while. I drink red wine to numb my brain and stop my thoughts so I can rest, but I can't sleep. I drink Cinzano, so much it makes me vomit, but still I can't sleep.

Gradually the sky grows paler. The shapes of houses and factories become more distinct. A cold dawn breeze rustles the leaves of elm trees down in the car park, carrying a drift of sweetness from the night-scented jasmine that clings to the brick wall of the building. The breeze chills my face as I sit huddled in my mohair rug. The city is waking, and at last my thoughts are starting to slow down. If I try to remember what I was thinking a minute ago, I can't.

I stagger to the bathroom, have a pee, and collapse on the bed.

*

Late morning. Another day. I sit at my table to write to Robert. Danny said to keep the letter short and as matter-of-fact as possible. But I decide to try and appeal to his better nature.

4 October 1972

Robert, I am still in a state of numbness – post-shock. I will recover but will never be the same again.

I keep wondering if I could have altered the course of events – could have made things go better. But I think whatever I had done, once I told you I didn't love you and didn't want to be your wife any more, it would have turned out badly.

I suppose what I did gave you the impetus to do what you did, but I don't see that you had justification for your action. I didn't want to abandon my children, as you put it. I've never wanted to leave them. You announced you were going to take a job in America but agreed to discuss access in a meeting with our two lawyers.

Now, I can't reach them, can't see them without your permission and only under your terms. And I have no money, no way of affording travel overseas.

Do you think they want this? They've been with me every day of their lives until that day I left for Sydney in May.

They may believe I don't want to be with them. They won't understand that it is impossible for me to see them unless you allow it. They may feel I don't love them. That's what I felt when my father left. And when he didn't contact me or try to stay in touch, I believed he'd never loved me. I believed I was unlovable. I believed it was my fault that he left.

Please reassure the children that I love them and want to see them soon. Please do not turn them against me. You have a tremendous responsibility, not for my sake, but for theirs. I have done wrong to you, I have hurt you, but I've tried throughout not to hurt you through or with them. That is why I agreed to leave them with you. Because I feared what you would do if I tried to take them with me, and because I didn't want them to be torn apart. You have tremendous power to hurt them and me – please don't.

Please don't leave me destitute. I think the sum I am asking for, six thousand dollars to see me through a Masters degree in English, is reasonable. Just enough to support me while I get some training for a career. I'm relying on getting another scholarship to pay the fees. I'm told I have a good chance of getting one. I've been a full-time parent for the past eight years and have no qualifications for work. The only jobs I can do are menial ones. I need a good job so that I can save money and travel to see the children. For those years we lived together as parents, I kept house, mothered the children, arranged our social life, supported you in your busy career, and was the children's main carer when you were at work and away at conferences and on visiting fellowships. Without me, you couldn't have had a family and a career, and done as well as you have.

I will send the children a tape as soon as I can bear to make one. I sent one to your parents' address last week, but it will now be a while before they get it.

Please give them all my love.

Anna

PS Please remember the delay in postage as well as a delay of anything up to two weeks in getting an overseas cheque cleared. Neither David nor my mother can afford to support me.

Twenty

I have nothing to live for but hope. I've put the children's paintings and drawings that I brought with me on the walls of the two rooms in this little flat. I have a mini tape recorder, and I record little snippets of my life on it, news of their Nanna, and some songs and stories. I bought a little book called *The Songs of Pooh*. It will be winter in Boulder soon, and they'll see snow again. So I record this little ditty.

> The more it snows (Tiddly pom)
> The more it goes (Tiddly pom)
> The more it goes (Tiddly pom)
> On snowing.
>
> And nobody knows (Tiddly pom)
> How cold my toes (Tiddly pom)
> How cold my toes (Tiddly pom)
> Are growing.

I work six nights a week at a wine bar café down the end of Darling Street near the wharf. It's in an old sandstone building, and the café is on three levels. It's hard and exhausting work. I started off with two nights a week and they've kept increasing it. I put in an application for a Commonwealth scholarship for an MA by coursework.

I haven't heard anything more from the States. Danny has found an American lawyer for me. The fee he's quoted is two thousand US dollars upfront, and more if necessary, depending on the amount of work needed. I have no way of paying for that, but Mum has offered to pay it for me. I feel bad about this, but she pointed out to me that it will come out of the trust fund that my uncle left in her name, to support her until her death and then to be divided between her children.

'I'll arrange it with David,' she said on the phone, 'and when I die, that amount can be deducted from your share of the estate.'

'Mum, thank you so much. I'm so sorry for all the worry and pain I've caused you.'

'Darling, I'm here for you, and so are David and Jo. You've had a terrible shock. Nothing can justify what he's done. He's clearly unbalanced, not to say vindictive and irresponsible. To take young children away from their mother is a crime. I don't know how he managed to get them out of the country.'

'Well, remember I told you he insisted I agree to them having separate passports before we left England? I think he must have foreseen that I wouldn't stay with him, and he plotted that if that happened, he'd get a job in the States and take them with him. If anyone queried him taking them out of the country without their mother, he probably said I was ill or something and would be following them later.'

'Good heavens! He must be very devious. And perhaps very afraid. Certainly very selfish. Not considering the effect on the girls, and their needs for their mother. Now, darling, is that all the money you need? What about Danny's fees?'

'Oh, Mum, he's doing my work for nothing. Maybe because I'm David's sister. When I protested, he said that twenty-five per cent of his work is pro bono, and that it is the least he can do for me.'

'Oh, what a good man!'

This morning, I received a package from Robert: some drawings done by the girls, and a brief note.

> Sophia and Caitlin have started school here, and Penelope goes to day care two days a week. My parents are coming over to live with us for six months, to care for the children until I find a reliable housekeeper.
>
> Re your access and a formal separation, I have discussed matters with a lawyer. He should be in touch with your lawyer soon.

I haven't heard anything from his parents. I'm sure they don't want to have anything to do with me. I can imagine what stories Robert's told them. I'll write and thank them for going over to look after the children. They're in their seventies, so it will be a big challenge for them.

*

I go in to uni see the Professor of Early English Language and Literature about some tutoring to keep me going until I get a scholarship (assuming I do). I was one of his pets when I was a teaching fellow.

He offers me a fill-in job for six months as his research assistant. 'That should see you through till the scholarship starts,' he says, puffing on his pipe.

It turns out to be a sinecure. I sit in the grey sanctuary of the library, looking through journals, writing down the titles and authors of articles in his subject area, making a half-hearted attempt at creating a card index for him. When I show him, he looks embarrassed and tells me not to worry: the money is there, not being used, and I might as well have it.

I've quit the waitressing job. I have to find ways to distract myself from my thoughts about the children. I've no idea how they're feeling, what they think about why I'm not with them, what Robert has told them. How are they finding the American school? Is Penelope happy at day care? Apart from her grandparents, she's never been looked after by anyone but Robert and me. Is Sophia still sucking her thumb? Have they got Bunny and Orange and Brown Teddy with them? Has Penelope got her blankie to sleep with?

I can't speak to them directly, only in letters and tapes. It hurts so much to make those recordings for them, but I try to keep it light-hearted, and let my voice carry my love for them. So, I make myself do it once a week.

David offers me some courier work, taking documents from his legal practice in the city to the court or to barrister's rooms. I do this for a while. Then I answer an ad for a party help. The jobs pay quite well, but by the time I get the train and the bus out to a posh address on the North Shore or the eastern suburbs, work on my feet for hours preparing food and serving it, then get a cab home if it's too late to use public transport, I am exhausted and not much better off. I decide that, like waitressing, it's not worth it.

Yet, I need to fill in my time. I live in suspension, not knowing when or if I'll see the children again. The days drift by and I do my best to keep occupied. I've started sketching again, but my heart's not in it. I try to read, but the words don't sink in. I go for long walks in Balmain, finding some solace in being amongst people who don't know me, don't know that my life is shattered. To them, I'm just a young woman going about my business.

A trunk arrives with some of my winter clothes and a few treasures in it. The trunk was in storage in Brisbane with all our household things from England, so he must have got the whole lot shipped to the States. Some of the things I carefully packed to remind me of our English home are not there. The gifts Mum gave us, some of my pottery and books. There are lots of spaces in the photo album that I'd put together before we left. He's taken all the photos of the children out, and our wedding photos. Photos of the girls since they were babies, of Sophia on the top of the slide in the garden, in tights and jacket and mittens, in our second winter there, with snow lying thick on the ground; of Caitlin sitting on the potty when she was about Penelope's age now; of Penelope in the baby chair in our VW bus, frowning because she didn't like being strapped in; of the three of them playing together outside the farmhouse, gathering the windfall of crab apples… Oh, how cruel! He could have easily got copies made to keep.

A letter came this morning; an airletter, addressed in his forward-sloping letters in blue ink. I know the moods of his writing so well. When he is tense or feeling the need to take control, his writing gets scrawlier, the loops more defined, the pressure firmer. I find a knife to slit the edge and open it out, my heart beating fast. He says,

> The children are settling well into their new life in Boulder. My parents will be here next week to keep the household going until I

can find a suitable housekeeper. Meantime, I go to work on the days that Penelope is in day care, and I work from home the other days.

Re access, I envisage that we can agree to you coming for three months within this coming year, preferably in the winter, when the children will have their long vacation. Then, in subsequent years, a minimum of one month a year if we can make suitable arrangements. It's too soon to go into detail. This will be worked out when we get a conversation going with our lawyers. As far as access is concerned, it is of course dependent on a formal separation that spells out terms re access and other matters. I am adamant that my rights as custodial parent of my children must be protected and respected. Your access is dependent on that.

I assume your lawyer has connected with a lawyer over here. I am seeing my lawyer tomorrow.

I write,

Dear Robert

I received the trunk yesterday. Everything was in good order. I was disappointed, however, to find that some of the things I expected were missing: some of my books, including cookery books, the ceramic vase in which I kept the dried flowers at Walnut Tree Farmhouse, and the ceramic lamp we got with my mother's money at the Woodshop. I was more upset to open the photo album and find only a few photos of my family in it. The photos of the children over the years are priceless, and a record of my life as much as yours. Would you please have as many of them as you can copied for me, as well as the wedding photos? Surely, it's more important for me to have photos of the children during those years than for you, since I'm the one separated from them. I have so little to remind me of them.

When you assumed the right to take custody of them, I trusted you would honour your promise to keep up my connection with them, to make it possible for me to see them. If you had found a post at an Australian university, they could have lived with me for long periods each year, alternating between me and you. Now you've reduced this to the possibility of three months this coming year, and one month in subsequent years if it can be arranged. This is not good enough. I never wanted to lose my children, and I object to the injustice of your idea that they're your children, and that you'll protect your home and ownership of them from me at all costs.

I've never behaved as a mother in a way that justifies this. You left me with no choice but to leave, by threatening me with murder and suicide. I love my children, and they love me, and you have no right to put so many obstacles between us. At every stage since separating, you've denied me the right to any say in their lives and their relationship with me. Please remember I gave you freedom from an incompatible relationship, as much as I have sought my own.

Up until the time you left Australia with the children without telling me, I felt affection and concern for you. You've destroyed that. The best that can be salvaged from the ruins of our relationship is cooperation, based on legal guarantees, over my access to the children. You're 'adamant' about protecting your 'rights'. I, too, am adamant. I need to have clear terms of access. One month a year is not going to sustain my relationship with them. Children have short memories, especially when they are very young, and in eleven months, I will fade from their minds, and they will find it very hard to keep the knowledge that I love them in their hearts.

I will not sign any agreement until I and my lawyer are satisfied that it gives me the best possible terms of access for my children's sake. I will not cooperate any further until I have them.

A week later, the post brings a draft agreement he wants me to sign. With it is a letter in his writing.

Anna, the terms in this agreement are the best I can offer. My terms are generous. I am willing to pay your return fares to Colorado and to provide accommodation while you are here. On your first visit, you will have three months with the girls, sharing their parenting. This is the maximum period you are allowed to stay on a visitor's visa. You will have to sign the enclosed separation and access agreement first. A divorce will follow in due course.

After your first visit, we will consider the timing and the length of your stay for the next visit. Do not ask for financial settlement beyond your fare and accommodation while you are here. My funds are tied up in the house I am buying, to provide a home for my children, and the costs of running the household and educating them. If you do not accept these terms, access cannot proceed.

Be assured the girls are happy here and settling in well.

I discuss it with Danny and write a reply.

I had hoped we could discuss together the issue of my access to the children before any binding legal document is signed. There are several points concerning access and custody of the children which I'm worried about, and it's difficult to communicate by letter. I don't want to threaten you, claim half the property bought with our joint money, try and get the children away from you, or any of the things you seem to fear. I'm not interested in my legal rights except in so far as they affect my bond with our children. I'm sure my interest in the marriage is no more than yours, and I have no interest in any property, whether yours or mine. I accept your word that the children are settling in well. But it is vital that their connection with me is maintained as well as possible, given that we are thousands of miles apart from each other. Please remember, when you threaten me by withholding access, you also threaten their happiness and mental health, and your own reputation for fairness in the eyes of the world. Should you attempt to do such a thing, there is no place where you could go to escape the guilt you would carry, and the harm done to the children. If, as you say, you really care about the children's happiness, the onus is on you to make it possible for them to see me…

You ended your letter with a threat. Surely you don't need to do that. This is not the only way we have of resolving these important issues between us.

Thank you for sending the children's school reports. I trust you'll maintain their contact with me, for their sakes, until a legal settlement is reached formalising the situation.

I have withheld from him all my fears, that he is absent a lot, with some substitute carer looking after them, that he is not emotionally available to them in their grief and confusion, not aware of the beliefs they may have formed that I don't love them and don't want to be with them... Worse still, that he's actually giving them that message. I fear that he is so wrapped up in his own turmoil of emotions – anger with me, desire for revenge, fear that he will lose them, that I'll somehow take them back from him – I imagine that he is going through a time of darkness, fear and doubt, trying to run the household, which he's never had to do before, and see to their needs, while his own needs are so out of balance that he's just managing to hold on. I can't say any of this to him. I have to speak to him as if he is capable of compassion and common sense and seeing things from the children's point of view.

The days pass and I hear nothing back from him. Perhaps he's waiting for his lawyer to review the agreement.

Twenty-one

It's hard to believe it's four months since Robert took the children to America last October. The days, weeks, months have passed in a grey blur. In May, it will be a year since I left them.

I don't really care what I do, nothing has any reality for me.

On Danny's advice, I go in to the American consulate to see about getting a visa. I walk up Martin Place to the multistorey building and get a lift up to the tenth floor. To enter, I press a buzzer.

A security guard comes out the double glass doors and nods. He asks my name and purpose for being there. 'ID, please, ma'am.'

I show him my passport. He scrutinises it, looks at my face, and hands it back. He waves me through to the desk.

I'm told to take a seat. There are several others ahead of me, and I resign myself to a long wait. I look at the others and wonder what their reasons are for wanting a visa. I don't imagine any of the women I see have three little children under the age of eight living there without them. No one can have a more urgent reason than I have for needing a visa.

I wonder what my girls are doing now? Sophia's birthday was last week. I sent her a soft toy, a platypus with silky soft dark brown fur and a grey-brown bill that feels like suede. And a tape with some stories and songs, plus a Beatrix Potter book for each of the girls. I wonder if she had a party. I wonder if she missed me. Her last birthday was in England, and she had her best buddy Jane, her sisters, and six friends from playgroup there, and a cherry cake.

'Miss Anderson?' the clerk calls, and I walk over to the counter. 'Go to the third cubicle on the left and wait there. An officer will be with you shortly.'

As the minutes pass, I try to breathe slowly and calm my racing heart.

A man walks in, short, middle-aged, balding. Unsmiling, he holds out his hand. 'Hi, Miss Anderson. How can I help?' His grip is loose, his fingers cold.

'I need a visa to visit my children. They're in Boulder, Colorado, with their father.'

'How come you're not with them?'

'Their father abducted them last October.'

He looks at me as if he's seeing me for the first time. 'Wow!' He shakes his head. 'How did he do that?'

'He forced me to leave them. We came back from England and were staying in a beach unit near his family in Queensland. We…we hadn't been getting on for quite a while. We quarrelled, and he forced me to leave them and go to Sydney – my family live here. He threatened me with murder and suicide if I tried to take them with me.'

He's silent for a few seconds. I wonder if he believes me.

'So what's happened since then?'

'My lawyer is helping me to try and get access. We've got as far as getting an American lawyer to talk with his lawyer on terms of access. But he's refusing to grant me access until I sign a separation agreement, and then he'll arrange a divorce.'

He shakes his head again and frowns. 'Miss Anderson, I'll take advice on this from the consul, of course. But I'm sorry to say you don't qualify to get a tourist visa.'

'Why not?'

'Because the terms of a tourist visa are strict. The maximum you can stay for is ninety days. And the fact that you have three children living there means there's a strong possibility you will want to stay. So, you might try to stay on illegally.'

'Can…can I have a glass of water please?'

He reaches for the carafe of water on his desk and a glass and pours me some.

I wet my lips and take a deep breath. 'So how can I get to see them? They're only eight, five and three years old. I haven't seen them for eight months!'

'As I said, I'll have to discuss your case with the consul. But I will ask you to write a brief statement of your circumstances and sign it – get it witnessed here by our clerk. I think your best bet will be to stay married, so you can apply for an immigrant visa.' He passes me a sheet of paper with the consulate letterhead and stands up, gesturing to the door.

'But…but if I'm still married to him, then I'd be able to stay on if we can agree on that. So, either way, I could stay on. Yet you won't let me have a tourist visa because I might stay on! That doesn't make sense.'

He sighs and looks at his feet, perhaps searching for an answer that will close this interview. 'Ma'am, I know it may seem that way to you. But from our point of view, if you're married to him and decide to stay on there legally, he is legally and financially responsible for you as his wife and the mother of his children. Whereas if you are formally separated or divorced and you stay on illegally, we'll have the trouble and expense of chasing you up and deporting you.'

I can't think of anything to say in answer to this. I meet his eyes, which are not as veiled as they were when we first began this. There's a glimmer of softness there. He's just doing his job, after all. He didn't make the laws.

'OK, thanks for explaining. So what do I need to say in the statement?'

'How long you've been married, what your husband's citizenship is, how old your children are, where they are living, and the fact that he took them out of the country without your knowledge or consent. Make your statement clear. We'll consider it and reply within seven days. We may then ask for supporting evidence.' He nods and opens the door for me.

*

I feel more stymied than ever. I'm in a catch-22 situation. Robert's refusing to give me access unless we're divorced, and the consulate is refusing me a visa if I'm not married to him.

After a few days, I get a phone call from the consulate asking me to go in for another interview. The same officer sees me.

'Mrs Anderson,' (so he's calling me Mrs, not Miss, this time!) 'I've spoken with the consul about your case, and he's read your statement. I can only repeat what I said before. But I'll try to put it more clearly. This is how it is. You have no hope of getting a tourist visa. As far as the immigration laws are concerned, to put it bluntly, you are guilty until you prove yourself innocent. That is, you have to prove to us that you have no intention of migrating to the US before we can grant a tourist visa. The fact that you have three children in the US would indicate an intention to stay there.' He pauses and looks at me.

I wait for him to go on.

'The only way you can get an immigrant visa is for your husband to petition us, and there is no way you can be granted one on the basis of his petition once you are divorced. The law is worded in the present tense. So long as you are not yet divorced, and you can produce a valid marriage certificate in support of the petition, the visa will be granted.'

I look at him. 'So what if we get a legal separation?'

He clears his throat. 'A marriage is still legal even if you are formally separated, and his obligations to you are still binding if you are within the jurisdiction of the United States. You could still go on an immigrant visa, as long as a divorce is not finalised while you are in the States. But you'd need a petition from him to support your application.'

'But...he's insisting on a divorce. So you're telling me I can't get an immigrant visa or a visitor's visa once we are divorced, if I return to Australia.'

'That would be a new case, and we'd have to consider it. But for your present situation, you may qualify for an immigrant visa as long as the divorce is not finalised while you are still in the States.'

My head is spinning. I feel like K in Kafka's *The Castle*, trying to find my way through the maze of bureaucracy. K wants to live legally in the village and the bureaucracy that rule from the Castle won't allow him to. Kafka died before he could finish the book but suggested it would end with K dying in the village, and receiving a letter on his death bed, saying that, although his legal claim to live in the village wasn't valid, certain 'auxiliary circumstances' were taken into account and he was permitted to live and work there. Too late.

I go home and write to Robert, explaining their terms and pleading with him to write a petition.

> The law is worded in the present tense. So long as we are not yet divorced, and you can produce a valid marriage certificate in support of the petition, the visa will be granted. It doesn't mean you are tied to me for life as long as you live there. A legal separation does not affect this since the marriage certificate is still valid. I asked if I could sign the divorce petition over there once the visa has been granted, and was told no, it must not be finalised while I am in the States.
>
> So the only way I can get access is for you to petition them and for us to remain legally married while I am in the States. Indeed, it seems that if we divorce while you live in the States, I may not be able to make any further visits.
>
> I know you don't want to accept this, but I'm afraid it's the only way I can come, and you can honour the agreement in regard to access. I can't apply for an immigrant visa in my own right, only as your wife. I'm enclosing a copy of the petition form for a visa, and I suggest you study it and write at once to the immigration consul here. He'll tell you directly what the situation is.
>
> You asked about my career and whether I will consider living in the States. As I said on the phone, it's important that we all have a chance to reassess the position. If it's possible, practically and emotionally, for me to be near the children. I should be near them. However, this is not a question that can be decided in the abstract. No firm or irreversible decisions can be made until I come over there and we all have a chance to work the problems out in the best way we can.
>
> Best wishes
> Anna

*

Meanwhile, another door closes. When Danny discussed my case with the American lawyer, he asked his opinion on the prospect of me winning custody in an American court. He replied that I'd got less than a fifty per cent chance of winning custody of them. Robert has possession, he has a profession, he has a house, and he's under American jurisdiction. I have nothing, no job, no money, no house, no future, I'm outside their laws, unable to go over there unless he cooperates. If I try for custody and lose the case, I'll have to pay costs. It's hopeless. I have to let him call the tune, and the best we can hope for is that he'll let me visit them at least once a year.

Twenty-two

I need to fill in my time and get a qualification so I can earn a reasonable salary. It's a challenge I've never come to terms with, being an independent, self-supporting woman. I married Robert while I was still a student, and I couldn't commit to completing a higher degree.

So why am I going back there? It's all I know how to do. I have the intelligence, I should be able to do it, and I quite like teaching. If I had a free choice, I'd do a degree in social work or social sciences, as I feel drawn to work with people who are disadvantaged. But I'd have to go back to being an undergraduate, and I wouldn't have a scholarship. It would take at least four years to qualify to work in the field, and I'd have nothing to live on during that time.

I'm granted another Commonwealth scholarship on the strength of my first class honours degree, so I've been given a second chance. It pays a small stipend, about fifty dollars a week, and I'm allowed to earn extra by doing some tutoring and marking exam papers. I can do a Master's degree by coursework, which should be a good start to getting a position teaching at uni.

I had no regrets about giving up academic life before. I felt like an impostor as an academic, and once I had my first baby, I just wanted to be a mother. It gave my life meaning, it felt real. Now I have nothing to live for. Whatever I do, I'm an impostor at life.

After Robert's phone call that dreadful October day, I've been phoning Danny every day. Mostly he's out or with a client. I keep calling until I get through to him. I am a junkie and he is my fix. He is always pleased to hear from me, warm and reassuring, and tells me to phone him again the next day. He doesn't complain about the multiple messages I leave with his secretary. I suppose the office staff are used to his female clients pestering him.

One morning, I wake from a dreamless sleep to his phone call. 'Anna, I'll be out your way late in the afternoon. There's an old lady I visit there, a client who can't get in to the city to see me. Can I call in and see your little flat?'

I know lawyers are not supposed to make home visits, especially to young female clients. I'm sure he does too. I tidy up the flat and walk down to the shops to get some fresh fruit and ground coffee, and shortbread from the deli on the corner; they make their own. I'm excited that he's coming to visit me.

At last, there is a firm knock on the door. He is dressed as always in business suit, shirt and tie. He holds out a bunch of tiny pink rosebuds, each one perfectly rolled and furled like a small, chubby cherub waiting to unfold and take flight. While coffee is brewing in the plunger, I take him on a ceremonial tour of the two rooms and balcony that comprise my little flat. We sit at the purple table and he offers me a cigarette. I let him light it for me.

Across the jangled patchwork of roofs and chimneys, the sun glints and dances on the harbour. I look away, my eyes dazzled by the light. I thought I'd never fall in love again, after Derek. Jack was an escape, a loveable one, but nothing more than that – no, that's not true. He was a catalyst for the break-up of my marriage. Neither of us foresaw that our weekend in Brisbane would lead to the loss of my children. He wanted it to be more than an escape, but he isn't free, he has a business and a family. He wrote to me for a while, and wanted to come down and visit me, or pay for me to visit him in Brisbane. But I said no. I don't want to be someone's escape from an unhappy marriage.

Once I got to Sydney and tried to find a way of getting access to the children, Danny became the person I could trust and confide in. When I met him, Jack and Derek faded from my mind. Danny hasn't replaced my children, but the thought of him stops me thinking about them all the time, helps dull the ache that is always there. He is my anaesthetic, my sedative, my narcotic. Without him, I would sink into despair.

'This coffee's good!' he says.

I pour him another cup.

'Have you heard any more from Robert or his lawyer?'

'No. I've written explaining the visa situation. The consulate won't grant me a visa unless he petitions them and we're still married, and he won't grant me access unless we're divorced. It seems hopeless, unless he gives in. But then, if I go over for a visit and return, unless we're still married, I probably won't be able to go back again.'

He takes my hand. 'I can only imagine how you feel. But I'm sure we'll find a way through.'

I sigh. 'We have to. I can't imagine going on living if I can't get access to them.'

'Oh, Petal, you will get access. It may be a cliché, but…where there's a will there's a way.'

I drain my coffee. 'I don't know why I married him in the first place. I was too young to know what I wanted. Then, my children gave it meaning. Now, that's broken.'

Danny leans back in his chair and looks at the girls' paintings on the wall. 'It's a common story. People marry young, they grow and change, and begin to realise they're tied into a contract that's very hard to get out of, especially once they have children. But you're still young, you've got a lot to live for, and you will see your children again.'

I wonder if he's thinking about his own situation. He hasn't told me anything about his private life.

He smiles his warm, reassuring smile. Then he looks at his watch. 'Time's escaped me again! I have to go. Thank you for letting me see your little nest. I wanted to see if you're comfortable and have everything you need.' He drains his cup and stands up.

Behind his kind words, I sense a desire for more contact, for intimate touching. I walk slowly to the door with him, my fingers touching his, making a wish for him not to leave me.

If only…in a sliver of late summer in a small flat, hidden from the eyes of my family and friends, from his world of the Law, the City and his family — if only we could suspend time, the judgements of others, his fears of overstepping his professional role, and meet as lovers. I can still hear his voice at the end of our first interview, ringing with strength. In it I heard the belief in my right to be free of the prison of my marriage, to be happy, to regain something of the all that I have lost. I still want to believe that that is possible.

Near the door, he turns and holds out his arms. Our mouths meet, our bodies fuse, we sink to the floor. Soon we are lying wrapped together, floating in a silvery swell on the harbour, now up, now down, twisting and turning like waves of light.

The union is brief, retreating with the tide. He adjusts his clothes, I slip on my pants and pull down my dress.

Morality returns; he apologises, he didn't intend this to happen.

He's gone. It will always be like this, I know. My life seems to keep repeating itself, a stuck record. I cannot have what I desire. I cannot have my children, I cannot have the man I love. I went wrong somewhere, way back. Perhaps in childhood, when I lost my father. Now my children are having to live what I lived. I was seven when he left, the same age Sophia was when we separated. But my childhood loss is multiplied three times in them. I feel as though I have died, but somehow I'm stuck in limbo, between worlds. A lost spirit. I need to make myself another life, but I don't know how to do it. I know Danny is not the answer, but I can't help hoping things will change.

*

I never know when he will come. We speak on the phone every day; he's given me his private number at work, so I call until he answers, or he calls me between clients, or from a public phone when he is out and about. I am lucky if I see him more than once a week, and I spend many days and evenings waiting in, in case he wants to call in. I get few phone calls, especially at night. I sit and try to read, sipping a glass of David's home-bottled red, on the alert for the phone to ring.

He works long hours, starting early, finishing some days at eight or nine p.m., and sometimes, after those late stints, he calls in with a bottle of beer and a bottle of red, and we spend an hour or two together.

Since that first visit, my days revolve around speaking to him. Just hearing his voice makes me feel better. And every now and then, he says what I'm hoping to hear: 'Petal, I'm on my way home soon. Can I call in and see you on the way?'

He plays squash sometimes after work and calls in after that. He used to be the captain of the Australian squash team, he tells me. 'I don't get time to play as much as I used to. But I still love it, it keeps me fit, after sitting in my office all day, and it helps me get work out of my head, smashing that ball into the wall.'

I wonder about his wife, how she feels about him working such long hours. I don't know what I mean to him, except that he desires me and loves my company. He's not said he loves me. I don't say it either, but I think it and feel it all the time I am with him. He says things like 'You've no sharp edges…you're a giver, not a taker…' Although he gives me no assurances, I feel that we belong together and I long to see more of him. He's living a double life, using me as an escape from all his duties and what I presume is an unhappy marriage. He gives me so much, and yet so little.

He makes no promises. My other two lovers did, and when it came to a choice, they couldn't keep them. I trust him and know he has my interests at heart. But still I hope that one day he will make more room for me in his life. In one way, I feel more anchored, in that I look forward to seeing him and forget my troubles when I'm with him. But in another way, it makes me feel even more in-between. I'm not a wife, I'm not a mother except in absentia, and I'm his 'other woman', with no official status, a secret to be kept between us. He's a lawyer, breaching his professional codes by having a relationship with me, and I'm the sister of one of his good professional friends. If I make myself look at it from an outsider's point of view, I can see that he's taking advantage of me. I'm vulnerable and helpless, and he's won my trust, but he's violating that trust by being my lover. I know that, and yet, he's my lifeline. My hope to be reunited with my children keeps me alive, and he gives my life warmth and meaning, even though it's in measured, irregular doses.

Sometimes, in bed, I lie awake and reflect on my life in the last couple of years. All those years I was with Robert, I yearned for a deeper relationship. I fantasised about other men and flirted with them at parties, but I didn't seek to have an affair. Even though Robert had affairs and told me about a couple of them, I sensed that he would not tolerate infidelity on my part. His theme, that he would do nothing to break up the marriage, rang hollow to me. It was only possible for him to say that because he had control. He was the income earner and provider, he came and went as he chose, he had freedom to do as he pleased when he was away from home. When I met Derek and yielded to his pleas, I knew I couldn't keep it up. I couldn't live a double life. Above all, I couldn't be Derek's lover and still have sex with Robert. My sexual role in our marriage had been mostly passive; I never sought sex with him, but when he sought it, I put on an act, I did the things that pleasured him and faked my own responses.

So how has it happened that I, who long for a stable, committed, equal and fulfilling relationship with a man, someone I can trust and give myself wholly to, have fallen from an unequal, exploitative marriage relationship into three affairs, one after the other, with men who are not available, two of whom swore that I was the love of their life, yet none of them have been able to give me what I am seeking? Is it like this for other women too? Why can I not find someone who will give me what I seek? Is the problem with the men, or is it my own insecurity and self-doubt, that leads me to give myself to men who will let me down?

I think of my father and when he left. My childhood ended that day. I became my mother's main helper, companion and confidante, and I had to bury my own grief and despair and listen to her diatribes against him. She unloaded her own grief and anger onto me, a seven-year-old child. As the weeks and months passed, and he didn't write to me or answer the letters and the Christmas parcel I sent to the address that Mum gave me, I killed him off in my heart. But his ghost lived on. The ghost of my desire to find someone who would fill that hole in my heart, would meet my longing for love and commitment. Someone who would not abandon me or just use me for their own needs.

And yet, I know, although he's careful not to say he loves me or to make any commitment, that Danny loves me in the way he is able to. That he really cares about me and wants to help me, and that he sees in me qualities that he admires in a woman. And that I give him some of the intimacy and joy that he may have sought in his marriage, but either has lost or has never had. Maybe it's commitment he has a problem with. Or is it that he feels committed to his family, and so can't make a commitment to me? Either way, he can't give me what I need, and yet, I'd rather have the little he gives me and long for more than have nothing.

Perhaps, in the perverse way that Freud describes, I am searching for my lost father, but because my father deserted me, I keep repeating that pattern, falling for men who will abandon me or who cannot give me what I desire. It's not sex I desire; that's just the vehicle for knowing, for giving, for receiving love. For me, it's the currency of love. I'm beginning to suspect that for men, sex is the primary object, and love is the secondary effect of having good sex. It's a game I've learned to play, but I keep losing at it.

Twenty-three

The balcony view of water and rooftops is too bright and cheerful, even by the light of a dying moon. I move into a little house at the grotty bottom end of Balmain, in a road that sweeps like an oily black snake up to Darling Street from Pyrmont and Glebe, past factories, docks and warehouses. A few grubby nineteenth-century houses line the street along the western side, yielding to shops and offices at the top end near Darling Street.

The house is three rooms long and one room wide, with a bathroom in a lean-to shed at the back. The back garden is a tiny strip overgrown with vines and shrubs, enclosed by a rickety old wooden fence separating it from a choked-up rear laneway. On one side of the house are drunks whose shouted curses float into my kitchen on the fishy evening breeze curling up from the docks. On the other side lives a shrivelled old woman. She emerges late afternoons and creeps to the corner shop, balancing on a knotted stick.

I am strangely comforted by being amongst people whose daily life is a practice of loss.

One Saturday, Danny breaks his usual routine of calling in to see me on his way home from weekday work. He's dressed in tennis whites. His body is firm and well-muscled, with curling dark hair on his legs, arms and chest. He is full of physical energy and in most ways my opposite. He seems to find relief in coming to see me. We fit well, never at a loss for things to say. Though he is not a deep thinker, we talk for hours, or as long as his time allows, about life, each other, our likes and dislikes. He is an average middle-class man, a model of private school education and professional ambition – what my family would call 'a good catch'. Yet he has a sensitivity and intuitive wisdom I miss in most of the professional men I meet.

But I only have a small part of him. I always want more.

He drains the last drop of beer and stubs out his cigarette. He draws me in close, then takes my hand, saying, 'Come on! Come and let me hold you next to me.'

We walk arm in arm to my bedroom and threw our clothes onto the trunk that holds most of my clothes. We stand close and kiss, then he pulls me down onto the mattress with him. We lie together for a long time, twining, untwining, moving, resting.

The bedroom is our world now, containing only us. Its walls are transparent, the ceiling disappears. We are suspended together by gleaming silvery threads, two separate beings held in one fragile web.

*

'Come on, Precious. Let's get up and have a coffee before I go.' He jumps up and begins to dress. 'I was due home hours ago. People will be wondering what's happened to me.'

He hardly ever calls me Anna now. It is 'Petal' or 'Precious' in more tender moments. When he first called me Petal, I felt like a little girl again. But he is not my father. Though he is eleven years older, he is my lover. I don't want to be his child. But I enjoy feeling safe and protected when I am with him. As for his wife, he always refers to her in the third person, as 'she' or 'people', never by her name. He told me they became engaged when he was a young articled clerk, still a virgin. He jilted her a week before the wedding date. After some months, he felt sorry for her and married her after all, but they've never been happy.

'I'm not a great fan of the institution of marriage,' he says as he sips his coffee. 'So many people I know are either making the best of a bad thing, leading a double life, or in the throes of an expensive and painful divorce. If I had my time over again, I wouldn't marry. My children are the most beautiful people on earth, so I suppose it's been worthwhile. But I don't believe in this "till death do us part" business. I don't know why people have to make a federal affair out of an attraction that doesn't necessarily last.'

I wonder if he's letting me know that our affair won't last. If I'm one in a succession short-dated affairs. But I think he's reflecting on his own marriage, perhaps on mine, and some of the people he's helped with messy divorces. He made a commitment years ago and has felt trapped since then. He has a choice, because he's a man. He can stay or he can leave. There's a price to pay either way. But I'm sure if he did leave, he wouldn't pay the price I've had to pay.

He drains his coffee cup and sits back in the old wooden swivel chair I bought when I moved here, his eyes focused on the honeysuckle vine outside the window. It is in full flower, and tiny birds no bigger than my thumb are darting in and out, sipping from the flowers.

'I don't know why it should be the most difficult thing on earth to admit it's over,' he goes on. 'I love that Paul Simon song that's on the radio a lot now…fifty ways to leave your lover! It always makes me laugh!'

'I certainly didn't find an easy way to leave. I should get a booby prize for the worst way to do it. Danny, why do you stay with her?'

'I was on the point of leaving six years ago, and she told me she was pregnant again. I could only presume it was mine. So I stayed.' He frowns, closing his eyes and creasing his forehead.

I wonder if she has affairs too? If she knows that he does?

'Do you think you'll ever find the right time to leave her?'

'I want to stick it out as long as I can, at least until the little one's older.'

'Do you and she still make love?' I want to know how he feels about her, what she's like.

He sits for a moment, eyes shut, closed off. I've gone too far.

'We sleep in separate beds, but sometimes I can't avoid it.' He stands up, reaching for the sweater he threw over the back of the chair when he arrived.

Does he mean he can't avoid his own urges or that she pressures him, and he gives in? I can tell from his tone of voice that he doesn't want to pursue that subject.

He leaves again. My house is empty. I pour the dregs from the coffee pot into my cup and sit listening to the muffled roar of traffic going past, fantasising about a time when he will stay.

*

One night, when I am expecting him to come and visit me and he doesn't, I get into my car and drive to his address. I looked it up in the phone book, knowing he lives on the North Shore; it was the only entry under his surname. His house stands at the end of a leafy drive, set back from the street. It has two storeys, surrounded by tall trees. His car is parked outside, and the lights are on in the house. I park at the end of the driveway in the street and walk through the trees, closer to the house, hoping to catch a glimpse of his life, of his wife, of him.

He's been so careful to cocoon me, to keep me separate, to keep his family life partitioned off. Once, in the early days when I was his client and not his lover, not long after I had that fateful phone call from Robert, I was so desperate for reassurance, I phoned his home number, and when a woman answered the phone I hung up. Another night, I phoned and he answered and gave me advice in a carefully professional voice, so I knew she was in the background listening.

Once we became lovers, I was able at least to keep within the lines he drew. Until now.

I stand, listening for sounds. I imagine his children, the little one tucked up in bed, sleeping, the older ones still doing their homework, or talking with their parents. What is he doing? Perhaps he and his wife are sitting together, watching TV, or perhaps he is watching a sports program, she reading a magazine or a novel.

The curtains are all drawn, and a dog starts barking. I retreat and drive home.

*

Ten o'clock one winter night he phones, his voice strained and husky. 'Hello, Petal. Did I wake you?'

'No, I'm still up. What is it? You sound stressed.'

'I can't explain on the phone. Can I come and see you?'

'Of course!'

Twenty minutes later, he arrives, a small overnight bag over his shoulder, two bottles of beer under his arm.

A grey pallor overlies his normally ruddy complexion. After we've drained the bottles and he's smoked two cigarettes, I am still unsure what has driven him to me, but I can tell he doesn't want to talk about it.

'I need somewhere to lie my weary head. Can I stay here tonight?'

After visiting the bathroom, he lies down in his underpants and singlet under the doona. When I return from the bathroom he is asleep. I lie close to him, wakeful through the night, savouring the smell and warmth of his body, my arm across his chest, holding him for the first time as he sleeps.

In the morning, he gets up at six o'clock, showers and dresses and shares a pot of tea with me in the kitchen. It is still dark, but the birds are chattering in the vines outside the window. His face looks more alive, but his eyes don't meet mine.

'I have to go, Precious. Thank you for letting me stay. I don't know what I would have done without you.' He stands up, tucking his shirt into his trousers and adjusting his tie.

'Danny…do you want to tell me what's happened?'

He bends down to retie one of his shoelaces and straightens up, putting on his jacket. He braces his shoulders and pushes up his chin. 'It's too sordid to bore you with, Anna. Someday I'll tell you about it. Right now, just knowing you're here is all the help I need.'

He bends to kiss me and squeezes his arm round my shoulders, letting his cheek rest against mine.

*

I am beginning to think it would be less painful to give up hope. To sink down into the deep green of the river, to let the water fill my lungs, to stay under.

Despite all the support and help he's given me, the free legal advice, the kindness and consolation, loving him makes me feel even more lost. I am more of an outsider than ever. I am the other woman, I have no status, I have to keep our love a secret, and try to find meaning in daily life without him. I wonder how other women (or men, for that matter) manage to carry on affairs while they are married. I guess it is easier for men to have a secret life, at least physically, because they aren't tied to the house like so many women are. I am a dismal failure at deception. But sometimes I wish I'd been able to lead a double life. Then I'd still be with my children, we'd still be in England, still in the farmhouse.

I wonder why I have this desperate need to be true to my feelings, to match the surface with what is within. It doesn't seem to be the way the game of life is played by most people. Because I don't play to the rules, I lost the game and lost my children as well.

Then again, I don't suppose Danny sees himself as winning the game. He plays between the lines of the rules, but at a huge cost.

As for Robert, he might have won the children and the money, but I wonder whether he wakes in the early hours of the morning sometimes and feels appalled.

Marriage, it seems, is not about love, nor about honesty. It is supposed to be, that's the story I was told, but it isn't true.

When I met Danny, I was in flight. He is my refuge; with him I feel at home, with nothing to hide. Yet he is also a stranger, part of a world I can't visit. I doubt I could be a part of it even if he wanted me to be. My feelings for him are so deeply marbled with loss and impossibility that the experience is more painful than anything except the loss of my children.

Twenty-four

It's early June, twelve months since we separated, and still nothing's settled. Each day, the prospect of seeing my children again seems further away. Robert's still refusing to agree to access unless we're formally separated and I've signed the agreement.

The postman blows his whistle, and I rush out to the mailbox. I brush the cobwebs away and open the lid. A small, padded bag, addressed in Robert's writing. I tear it open. Inside is a cassette tape, enclosed in a piece of paper. He's scrawled a message on it.

> My parents left last week. We have a good housekeeper, Mandy, and the children are happy and settled. R.

This is the first tape I've had from the children this year. The last one was before Christmas, when their grandparents were still there. I put the tape in the cassette and turn it on.

Sophia's voice. 'Mummy, hello. We're on holidays now and Daddy's taking us to see *Robin Hood*! And our new housekeeper is Mandy. This morning we made choc chippies. They're yummy.'

She tells me about the class she's in, her teacher, how she walks to school each morning with her friend Marilla. I try to focus on what she's saying, but tears are rolling down my cheeks and I haven't got a hanky. I wipe my nose with my shirt and rub my hands across my eyes. Her voice is as I remember it, but she's rolling her *r*s and stretching her vowels.

'Goodbye, Mummy darling, I love you, and we miss you so much.'

I turn the tape off and run to the bedroom and throw myself on the mattress and cry. My pillow is soaked. I open the trunk my clothes are in and pull things out until I find my hankies.

Back in the kitchen, I open a bottle of wine and pour a glass, then turn the tape on again.

'Mummy, it's me.' Caitlin's voice. 'When are you coming? Daddy told us you'll be here for Christmas, but that's so far away! I'm in Grade One, and my teacher's name is Miss Marsh, and she's lovely. And we're going to see *Robin Hood* this afternoon.'

More news about her friends and the games they play. She hasn't picked up the American twang like Sophia has.

I hear Penelope's voice in the background, wanting to have her turn. 'Let me talk to Mummy!'

They squabble for a minute or two, until Sophia intervenes and tells Penelope she'll get her turn in a minute.

When Penelope comes on, she is lost for words at first. I hear her breathing in little grunts, then 'Um…Mama…when are you coming?' She pauses, as if waiting for my answer.

Sophia prompts her to tell me about her preschool and her friends.

'My friend is Peter. He kissed me yesterday, Mama!'

She's nearly three and a half now. A little girl, no longer a baby. She was still a baby when I left, walking, talking a mix of her own words and English, still wearing trainer pants. Caitlin was six in May, and Sophia was eight in February. How do they get to sleep at night? Does their father or Mandy read them stories, cuddle them? Do they share a bedroom? Do they get lonely? Do they lie awake sometimes and cry for me? Does Caitlin still wake up during the night and want to be cuddled back to sleep? Does her father hear her if she calls him?

At the end, they sing me a little song, a few lines from *The Wind in the Willows*…

> All along the backwater, through the rushes tall,
> Ducks are a-dabbling, up tails all!
> Ducks' tails, drakes' tails, yellow feet aquiver
> Yellow bills all out of sight, busy in the river…

Caitlin's voice is throaty, Sophia's softer, and Penelope trails behind the others, like a little bell chiming in the wind. I sent them *The Wind in the Willows* with the lovely original illustrations by E.H. Shepherd for Christmas, and a tape, on which I sang the whole of that song. I know it by heart because I played Mole in the school production of *Toad of Toad Hall*.

I finish the wine and go and lie on my bed. I don't want to think, I don't want to feel. I just want to go to sleep, to switch off. I can't be with them, they're stolen from me, I can't hold them and kiss them, I can't buy them new clothes when they grow out of the ones they have, I can't smell their hair, can't cuddle their warm, soft bodies, can't bathe and dry and dress them, can't laugh and play games with them.

I want to die. I could get some sleeping pills from the doctor and take them with a bottle of wine and go to sleep and never wake again. If I had a bath, I could lie immersed in the water and slit my wrists and pass out. No one would know. It would be days before anyone would find me.

I bury my head under the pillow to block out the drone of traffic on the street outside.

Twenty-five

It's Sunday, and I'm driving across Gladesville Bridge on my way to a wine bottling at David's house. A heavy weight sits in my chest and nothing shifts it. I start to cry and I can't stop. When I get to David's house, Jo opens the door, takes one look at me, and leads me by the hand upstairs to their bedroom.

'What is it, Anna? What's happened?'

'Nothing…it's just…I had a tape from them on Friday. They're happy over there, they're living their lives without me, they're growing up, and I'm not there, and I don't know when I'll see them again!'

She sits me down in the old green velvet armchair by the window. 'Wait a minute.' She disappears. She returns with two glasses of wine. She sits opposite me, perched on the end of the bed. 'I think you need to see a counsellor, Anna. You need to talk to someone who's not part of the family, who can help you deal with this impossible situation. You've done very well so far, but really, I get the feeling you're at the end of your tether.'

'I am,' I sob. 'I don't know when I'll see them again, I can't get a visa, Robert keeps making threats and trying to force me to agree to his terms, and the lawyer that Danny found for me over there says that I've got less than a fifty per cent chance of winning custody of them. He has possession, he has a profession, he has a house, and he's under American jurisdiction. The US consulate won't give me a visa unless I'm still married to Robert, and Robert's refusing to grant access unless I'm divorced. I have nothing, no job, no money, no house, no future, outside their laws, unable to go over there unless he cooperates. If I try for custody and lose the case, I'll have to pay costs. It's hopeless. I have to let him call the tune, and the best we can hope for is that he'll let me visit them at least once a year!'

'Darling, try not to despair. It's one step at a time. You should be eligible for free counselling as a postgraduate student. Let me make some enquiries. I'll ask James.'

James was her first husband, a psychiatrist. He's now a professor of psychiatry at Sydney Uni.

A couple of days later, she rings me and tells me to contact a guy called John Chapman. 'James says you'll be in good hands.'

*

A week later, I sit facing a heavily built man, a bit older than me, maybe forty, with bushy eyebrows, unkempt collar-length hair, and intense brown eyes. I tell him a short version of why I'm there, and he makes a few notes.

He looks up and gazes at me for a minute. 'You're in a helluvva situation. How do you feel about it?'

'Huh! How do I feel? There are no words for it. But recently…I've felt like dying.

'How would you do that?'

'Take pills and alcohol…I don't know. I don't have a plan. I just don't want to live.'

'So what's kept you going so far?'

'Hope. And I'm beginning to lose that.'

'Hope keeps people alive in impossible situations. So hold onto that. We need to work with your feelings. Beneath the hopelessness, the numbness, you've got a lot of grief and anger locked up inside you. Am I right?'

I look at him and become aware again of that rock in my chest. It never shifts.

'So what can I do about it?'

'Let's take it little by little. I can help you start to unlock those feelings. So that you have a bit of room to live with yourself and other people. Right now, you're ready to deck the next guy who says boo.'

I glance at him sideways, surprised. Is that really how I come across? Then I remember a male friend saying to me, 'You're an attractive woman, Anna. But you have an embattled look. You look as though you want to fight someone.'

'Who are you thinking of? Who do you want to fight?'

'Of course, Robert. I wanted to kill him that night he gave me the ultimatum about leaving the children with him. Then, when I saw how much pain he was in, I pushed that thought away. But it didn't go away, it settled in my chest.'

'So that's the rock. It's hatred, anger, the desire for revenge.'

He pauses, and I focus on the rock. Thoughts of my father surface. Leaving without saying goodbye, just walking away, never writing to me, never trying to make contact with me.

'What are you thinking of now?'

'My father. He left when I was seven years old. I didn't see or hear from him again until forty years later, when I wrote to him.'

'Ah. Loss behind loss. I want you to lie back in the chair, close your eyes. Focus on your breathing. In, out, nice and slow.' His voice drops and slows. 'In to a count of four, out to a count of six.'

He stops counting, and I lie, breathing, letting my thoughts drift.

His voice starts again, talking me through my body, from my toes up to my head. I feel a little softer, but there's still a hard lump inside me. It's shifted down to my belly.

'What are you feeling now?'

'The lump's moved down to my belly.'

'Describe it to me.'

'It's round and hard and heavy.'

'If you could give it a physical expression, some movement or gesture, what would you do?'

'I'd scream.'

'OK, so hold that thought. Take your consciousness down to your belly, let yourself merge with that hard, heavy lump. Don't make an enemy of it. It's part of you, old grief, new grief, old anger, new anger… it has a reason for being there. It wants to be released. Breathe deep, breathe down into it.'

For a few minutes, he gets me breathing deeply, feeling the lump, focusing on it, not trying to push it down harder, letting it rise up slowly through my belly towards my chest…

'You can scream, Anna. It's safe to scream. Let the scream out.'

*

After the scream, a little more soothing talk from him, and another appointment made, I walk out and catch a bus home in a daze. Nothing has changed, but I do feel lighter, a little more hopeful. And when I get home, I pick up the phone and ring Mum. I haven't talked to her lately about how I'm feeling, only about the tos and fros with Robert and the American consulate.

'Mum, I had a tape from the girls about a week ago.'

'Oh, how are they? What's happening?'

I give her their little bits of news, and we laugh a little and cry a little. It feels good to be able to share my feelings with her now. I've been very wary because I know she worries a lot about me and them, and her worry feels like a weight on me. When she is in her worrying mode, it takes me back to childhood, to the days, weeks and months after Dad left, and how she used me as her wailing wall. I felt frozen then, because I had my own grief and anger and despair, but I couldn't express it to her. She had no one else to talk to but me, most of the time. So I got used to just listening and pushing my own feelings down.

But now, when I tell her how I've been losing hope lately, she talks positively.

'Darling, I know they'll come back to you.'

'How will they? How do you know that? He's not going to let them go.'

'No, probably not. I don't know how I know, I just do! Somehow, I don't know how or when, they will come back to you.'

This makes me feel better. Mum has sixth sense, but doesn't like to talk about it as she is so rational. She's told me about several experiences she's had when she remembered scenes from past lives, or could see what was going to happen to her in this life.

My mother, the hero. She never gave up. So, when she says they will come back to me, I believe her.

After a few more sessions, I stop seeing the counsellor, as I feel he has nothing more to teach me. But we stay friends, and I talk to him on the phone sometimes, or meet him for coffee.

I've broken into that rock in my chest and started to release the grief and the anger. Now, at least when I am home alone, I feel a little more human, less like the walking dead. But my life is still a shell and I could shed it any time were it not for my daughters. Will it ever change? I can only keep going, and hope that it does, that I will be able to see them again, that I can make some sort of a life for myself.

Twenty-six

Negotiations with Robert are still in a cul-de-sac. He's insisting I sign the divorce petition before I visit the children, whereas the consulate maintains I can only get a visa if I'm still married to him. I'm stymied. No way forward, no way back.

It's October already, and still no agreement with Robert. The year is escaping me and I'm beginning to lose hope of seeing the children at Christmas time. Danny is still my consolation and my lifeline, but as busy and elusive as ever. He's made it clear to me that he has no hold over me. Between the lines, I read that he wants to keep being my lover, but he doesn't expect me to be faithful to him, he wants me to have a social life, to be as happy as I can, to see other men if I want to. I do take a lover occasionally, someone I am friends with, but it's just going through the motions for me, more because they want it than because I do. I am a one-man woman. I can't enjoy sex for its own sake. I have to be in love. That was my downfall in my marriage. It seems to be easier for men to separate the two.

When a friend asks me to a party, I say no at first. But then I think, there's no point staying at home on my own, waiting for Danny to visit. So I accept.

*

There are quite a few people here already. I feel uncomfortable and wish I hadn't come. I decide to avoid introductions and small talk. I accept a generous glass of red wine and spread a slice of crusty bread with hummus. I wander out to the terraced back garden and, from the upper level, catch glimpses of the harbour and wharf where ferries call on their way to and from the city. There is a knot of people standing near the veranda, but I don't know any of them, so I move over to the edge of the stone wall that drops down to the lower terrace. I can smell the night-scented jasmine that twines around the old brick toilet, and the sweet-sour scent of new-mown grass. The lights of the city are glimmering in the satiny water of the harbour.

'Hi.' The voice comes from behind me.

I turn to face the stranger, a tall man with dark eyes, olive-brown skin, and a thick crop of curly silvery-grey hair. His one word of greeting tells me he is American. His name is Richard.

I tell him I'm feeling antisocial tonight, and when he asks why, I hesitate, resenting his blunt curiosity. He's probably doing a line for me, but I don't want another man in my life.

The anonymity of the night, the faint seaweedy smell from the harbour, wash over me as the breeze touches my face. Should I tell him? Why not? He seems friendly. Sometimes it's easier to talk to a stranger than to someone you know. I walk over to a bench under the mulberry tree and sit, and he follows me. I begin to tell him about Robert's abduction of the children, my stalemate with him, the consulate's refusal to give me a tourist visa, my despair.

'Wow! You've sure had a hard time.' Richard takes a long swig from a can of beer. 'Maybe I can help you.'

'How? You're not a magician.'

'No, I'm not, but I might be the next best thing. Come on, let's dance. We can talk some more later.'

He's a good dancer, and we drink and dance till after midnight.

'Would you like to come home with me?' I ask.

'I sure would, babe. Haven't had so much fun for months.'

In my little kitchen we sit and have a last drink.

'How come you're out alone?' I say, draining my glass. 'A handsome man like you...'

'Ah well, it started last year. My wife's French, and she's gone to the Bahamas with a wealthy dude on his yacht. We'd been together twelve years, and we've got a ten-year-old boy.'

'Are you still in love with her?'

'Yeah, I guess I am. But I doubt she'll come back. She likes the high life, and Sydney's a bit tame for her.'

We go to bed, both more than a bit drunk. We kiss and stroke each other for a while, and he rubs his hips over mine, fumbles with my clitoris and kisses my nipples. Nothing more happens, and he falls asleep. I lie for a while, glad we haven't had intercourse, and wondering where this will go.

We sleep for maybe three or four hours, then he jumps out of bed and goes to the bathroom. In the kitchen, over a pot of tea, he tells me he has to get home. His son will be wondering where he is; he has a live-in housekeeper, but this is the first time he's stayed out all night.

'Anna,' he says, sipping a cup of strong black tea, 'I'm sorry I was a bit hopeless last night.'

'Oh, we were both drunk! I had a lovely evening with you, and thanks for cheering me up. Richard, you said you might be able to help me. What do you mean?'

'It's simple. I can get you a tourist visa. I'm the American consul. Didn't I mention that?'

I sit in silence. I spent the whole night with him and he didn't tell me that! Maybe he kept it as a surprise. We had such a good time dancing, he might have forgotten about it. It's hard to believe that I met him by accident and he turns out to be the one person who can help me with the mess I'm in.

'So just make an appointment to see me – I'll let the receptionist know to give you a priority appointment, as my appointment book is full – and I'll have the forms for you to sign.'

'Oh, Richard, I don't know what to say. You're an angel.' Perhaps it's not an accident we met. Perhaps he is a guardian angel in disguise.

'Kid, it's easy. It's your lucky day. Now, I need to tell you something.' He drains his cup and takes a deep breath. 'Y'know how nothing much happened last night. Well, I'm impotent. I have been since my wife left. I've been to a psych and he tells me that it's a nervous condition. Once

I've got my emotional life on track, he reckons I'll be OK. Is it a problem for you?'

'Oh, not really, I'm… I don't really want a hot love affair. My life's too broken at present. I don't know what I want.'

'You're a sweet woman. Can I visit again, maybe take you out for a picnic or a drive in the national park?'

'I'd love that. But let me come in and see you first and get that visa application in…not that I'm making that a condition, it's just that I want to get it sorted so I can get an access agreement with my husband and get to see my girls at Christmas time.'

It's as easy as he said it would be. The application goes in and, within a week, it's approved.

Richard visits me twice a week, bringing a bottle of French wine or Florfino sherry and a bunch of flowers. We go for drives and picnics in the forest, or walks along the cliffs, beaches and rock pools around the harbour. When he brings me home, sometimes we go to bed, but we never get past kissing and cuddling. I like him, he's charming and easy to talk to and good fun, but he's a diversion for me, from my anxious waiting, from my aching love for Danny, from the emptiness of my life. He is a means to an end, and I know it won't last.

Once I tell Robert that the barrier to my visit has gone, he sends me a legal notice of separation to sign, and a letter from his lawyer outlining terms of access. It states that I will have right of access in December this year and will be able to remain for three months. I will be provided with accommodation and he will pay my return fare, but I must support myself while I am there.

It's hard to believe it will actually happen. I talk to Mum about it, and she says she wants to come with me. She'll also help me financially. I have to take a few hundred dollars for each month I stay there, and I can't stay more than ninety days, under the terms of the visa.

I'd rather go on my own, as I'm not sure how Mum will bear the winter cold there, and what sort of accommodation we'll have. I don't want to feel responsible for her. But I know she wants to give me her support, and I guess she will be a buffer between me and Robert, since he respects her and will perhaps behave better with her there.

When I've signed and returned the papers and written to Robert saying that Mum will come with me, he writes back.

> Anna, you and your mother can stay at my house during the week, and I will stay with my girlfriend Kate. Then at weekends, you will stay in Kate's house and she will stay with me at my house. So, you will have all week with the girls, and I will have weekends. I'm sure you will agree this is a generous arrangement and will save you having to travel each day to see the children.

I discuss it with Mum and with Danny, and we agree that this is the best offer I am likely to get.

Robert's paying my return fare and giving us free accommodation. I don't want to stay in his house, but as long as he's not there when we're there, it's what I have to do. At least I'll be with the girls most of the time. It's the best I can get, and anything will be better than this empty life I'm living.

Twenty-seven

It's early December, late morning. Mum has closed her book and her eyes – she doesn't like landings and take-offs. The plane is descending over the Rocky Mountains, bumping through the turbulence. I gaze out the small window, craning my neck to see the earth. On the mountains, snow thaws on sharp-edged boulders, twisted bushes are etched in black. Above the snowline, aspens shiver, cloaked in white, and higher still, the firs are sharp and dark above the blue- and grey-shadowed snow. The ploughed wheat fields in the morning sunlight are striped with cinnamon, cocoa, maroon and indigo.

It's nineteen months since we separated at Mackay Airport. I've lost nearly two years of their life. I wonder how it feels for them, what they're thinking. I try not to think, just to wait, empty, holding the space in my heart, waiting for them to see me, to know me, to feel me. Waiting to hold them.

We take a cab to a gabled house in a street below the wall of mountains. The light stabs my eyes as it reflects off powdery snow covering the sidewalk and gardens. There they are, three small figures standing awkwardly in a row on the front doorstep. Sophia's long hair, parted in the middle, shows her pale, broad forehead; her hands pick at each other. Penelope, in the middle, clutches her white cardigan; her white blonde hair sticks out like a bush around her round face. Caitlin's hands are clasped, her knees turned in, her feet splayed, her mouth tucked into a half-smile.

They all look anxious and uncertain as they watch me open the cab door and climb out. I run up the path, leaving Mum to pay the driver. I drop my handbag as I kneel down and reach out my arms to hug all three of them. We cling together, our foreheads touching.

Do not speak, because if you do, you will scream or cry. What are they thinking, my little girls?

'But Mother – where have you been?' Penelope pulls back.

I meet her eyes, seaweed-green. I have no answer. I hug her closer to my breast.

Caitlin burrows her head into my neck, and makes a noise, something between a sob and a cry of joy.

Sophia strokes my face, and her tears spring onto my cheek.

My knees are turned to ice, I cannot move. We will become a statue, frozen at the threshold of his house, together but not living, because we cannot live together.

I make myself come back to life. I kiss each child on the eyes and cheeks to melt the frozen tears and straighten up, picking up my bag and its contents, which have spilled in the snow. After the driver brings our bags up to the door and Mum greets the girls, we climb the steps. Penelope's hand is tucked firmly into mine, Caitlin and Sophia are holding their nanna's hands. We cross the threshold of the home that is theirs but not mine.

'Where's your father?' I ask as we walk into the living room.

'He's in his study,' Sophia replies. 'He said he'd wait till you arrive, then go to Kate's house.'

I hear his footsteps. Firm and measured. He walks in and greets Mum, nodding at me. He's put on weight; his face has filled out. He's given up the pretence of covering the top of his head with the thinning hair. It's shaved, leaving a fringe of grey-ginger hair around the sides. He's added a beard to his moustache. The moustache matches his hair, but the beard is grey. His voice hasn't changed…a tenor, nasal, with a rising intonation. He doesn't make eye contact with me and busies himself with showing us round the house. Mum's bedroom is on ground floor level, and mine is in the basement, near the girls' rooms.

'Your room is normally the housekeeper's room,' Robert explains. 'But she's visiting her parents in Utah, taking a holiday while you're here.'

Sophia has a room of her own at the end of the corridor, and Caitlin and Penelope share a room next to mine. Their rooms are plain and functional, with furnishings that look as though he picked them up at some second-hand place. He's never been one for home-making, apart from the basics. It was always me that did that.

I focus my attention on the girls. I just want him to go. They cling close to me, and he keeps his eyes on them. I wonder if he is jealous over sharing the home he has made for them with me. How strange it is.

He turns towards me, looking at the floor. 'Normally, the girls would be at school and day care today. But I've arranged for them to start their vacation early. It's Monday, so you'll have the rest of the week with them, and I'll come back on Friday afternoon and take you to Kate's house. She's kindly letting you and your mother stay there each weekend.'

At last, after explaining the security system ('State of the art,' he says proudly) and the rubbish arrangements, and pointing out the bus timetables and town maps, he hugs and kisses the girls, picks up his suitcase and briefcase from the hallway, and leaves.

Mum looks in the kitchen cupboards and checks out the fridge. 'They're fairly well stocked. I need a cup of tea. Do you want one?

'No thanks, Mum.'

She fills the electric jug and looks for tea and cup. 'You go ahead and look around with the girls,' she says, 'and I'll make us some sandwiches for lunch.'

'Mummy,' Sophia pulls my hand, 'come and see our playroom.'

I follow the girls downstairs into a large, low-raftered room. There are beanbags, a few board games and a Yamaha keyboard at a big table, a bookcase with some story and picture books in it. Otherwise, it's pretty bare. The curtains are thin and don't fit the windows properly.

I'm at a bit of a loss what to do. I feel like a visitor in a house that doesn't know me, that's absorbed its owner's persona, functional and businesslike. I'd like to make it homely and inviting for them, but I can't do much while I'm here. There's a divan bed with a few old cushions on it. I ask them to find a story each, and we sit down, Penelope on my lap, her sisters snuggled in either side of me.

I have to get to know them again. I want to know about their daily lives, how they like living here, what they do when they're not at school, what their teachers are like… So many questions, but I have to wait and let them gradually lead me into their space again, not make them feel like I'm cross-examining them. I want to know, most of all, if they're happy, if they miss me, if they are getting enough love and attention. But I must let them show me little by little. Robert has told me so little about them. I don't know how he managed with them on the long journey here, how he's looked after them and kept his job going as well, how he fed them and managed their daily lives before his parents came… So many questions. I'll never know. There's a black hole there, nineteen months of change and growth and daily life, lost. For them, I think, they live in the present, and may not even think about that time. They may not remember much of it.

I am their mother, but I do not belong here. I must wear the mother's mask, act as normal as I can, calm, happy, loving, present. But inside, the mother that was me is shrunken, small like them, unsure of anything except this crushing pain of loss and longing. And to numb it, I must act, I must pretend that everything is all right, that we are a normal family, that I have never left them, that they are not lost to me.

I can't ask them how they felt in Mackay when they realised their father wasn't going to let them see me again, how they felt when he packed their stuff and took them onto the plane. How he explained it to them. If he told them I didn't want to be with them. Did he give them a choice? Did he ask them whether they wanted to be with me? If he did, I'm sure it would have been in such a way that they would feel he couldn't live without them. I recall his words: 'If you try to take them from me, I'll kill them, kill you, kill myself.'

So here I am in their lives, a ghost of the mother they knew. They don't know me now. I have changed, died and made myself live again, and though my love for them has never faded, it is bruised and tender and always mixed with grief. I can never go back to how I was with them, to the children I lost for nearly two years. They have grown and changed, and their lives don't revolve around me any more. I have to get to know them as they are now. Only to lose them again.

As for Mum, she slips back into the role of grandmother, doing little domestic chores like washing up, helping me cook meals, reading to them at bedtime, listening to Caitlin and Sophia read. She even makes a cake to celebrate our visit, a cherry cake with glacé cherries and icing. The girls attach themselves to her readily, though I'm sure they would only have patchy memories of her visits to us in England, and for Penelope, she was like a stranger at first. But she has such a comfortable way of being with them and loves talking with them and telling them stories, she fits like a familiar glove on a hand, warm, comfortable and safe.

Perhaps her accompanying me on this visit is a way of saying sorry for her judgement of me after I left them; even for having pushed me into marrying Robert in the first place. She doesn't speak about it, but I feel that she sees now how unsuited we were, how trapped I was in the marriage. She loved my father even when he behaved so badly and left us, and I think she went on loving him till the day she died. It was a love match in the first place. As she said in her handwritten memoir, she and he were accepted everywhere, from the beginning, as destined to marry, 'and we accepted it ourselves; it had a fatal inevitability about it, although he had no prospects'. Robert had prospects aplenty, which was the main reason she wanted me to marry him. I don't think she considered whether I loved him or not, whether we were compatible.

Twenty-eight

In Robert's house, during the hours the girls are awake, I act like a normal mother, and keep busy when I'm not cooking or looking after them by doing crochet and embroidery. I am making a shawl for Mum in creamy wool, with an elaborate border of flowers in purples, dark reds and pinks. The pattern is wrong, and as I sit at night unpulling and reworking sections, I think of all the steps that have brought me to this place, all the choices I made without realising the consequences. I drop the crochet sometimes – will I ever finish it? – and creep into their bedrooms. I bend over them as they sleep, watching their faces, uncreased and innocent, and inhale their sweet breath.

When I tire of the wayward shawl and the repetition of the pattern, I turn to another piece of work, an embroidery for the girls. Under my fingers, slowly, a picture grows of forest foliage with a faun's face peeping out, and words from The Song of Solomon: '…the time of the singing of birds is come, and the voice of the turtle is heard in our land'.

One afternoon, Mum and I take the girls shopping. We visit the supermarket to get a few things for dinner.

Mum doesn't say much. She turns to me as we walk out. 'America is a decadent nation of people. Where else would you see women in the supermarket in slippers and curlers, with cigarettes hanging out of their mouths? Buying Coke and cigarettes and junk food?'

We walk towards the entrance to the mall, and I stop in front of a haberdashery.

'Let's go in here, I want to make some clothes for you,' I say to the girls.

There's a portable sewing machine in the playroom. They help me choose the material, bright summer prints, and some patterns.

'Mum, will you help me with these? If I do the machining, can you do the hems and buttons?'

'Of course, I'll be glad to.'

She used to make all my clothes when I was little, on the old Singer treadle. When I was about twelve, I made my first dress, and after that, I made most of my clothes, as Mum's usually turned out too big for me.

Sophia runs over to a stand of curtain materials. 'Oh, look, Mummy. You said you don't like the curtains in the playroom. Will you make us some new ones?'

'Of course, darling. Let's choose a nice bright one.'

We find one in bright greens, yellows and reds, with fauns leaping amongst tangled vines and trees, and take it to the counter.

The shop assistant smiles at me and the girls. 'Hey, that's a neat coat you're wearing,' she says to me. 'What kinda fur is that?' She leans forward and fingers the cuff.

'Kangaroo,' I reply.

'Really! Did you shoot it yourself?' She chuckles. Then she turns to Mum, who's standing behind me, holding Penelope's hand. 'Hi, ma'am, how are you today? I love your hat! So cute. Is your day going well?'

No one wears hats here. Mum wears a grey felt one with a feather and the brim tucked in at one side. She buys a new hat every season, and never goes out without hat and gloves.

Mum replies, 'Yes, thank you,' in frosty tones. She speaks in polite 'standard English', with an undertone of condescension.

After treating the girls to drinks and cakes, we head for the bus stop. Mum chooses a seat near the front, and Caitlin sits beside her. I take the one behind, Penelope on my knee, Sophia at the window.

Mum turns round and complains in a low voice about the bad manners of these people. 'How impertinent! Commenting on my hat, fingering your kangaroo-skin coat, asking you what sort of animal fur it is!'

The man sitting in front of her turns round, and says, 'Say, lady! That's a neat accent! Where are ya from?'

She gives him a hard stare and turns back to me. 'Will you cut out the dresses or the curtains first?

Mum helps me cut out the dresses and pin them, and when I have sewn them, she does the hand finishing, the hems and buttons, and helps me hem the curtains.

At night, when the girls are asleep and Mum has gone to bed, the numbness returns. I drink red wine and sit listening to music until at last, sleep seems possible. In the morning, I look in the mirror and see my face, the face of a woman older than me. The lines under her eyes and round her mouth are sharply etched by the dry mountain air, cold winds and lack of sleep. I can't stay here. I will dry up and wither away before I grow old.

I have no space of my own. Nor does Mum, but that doesn't seem to worry her. She just gets on with life in her stoical way, as if we are back in Sydney and the girls are on holiday with us.

When Kate arrives, the first Friday afternoon when we're to make the changeover, she walks in, quick steps, definite manner, head held high. She is English, with a clipped accent and a high-pitched, creaky voice, as if she has sharp rocks in her throat. She's very businesslike, a little abrupt, but pleasant enough. She shakes hands with us both, then greets the girls. She has a way of asking questions with a falling intonation, as if she doesn't expect an answer.

'Welcome. I hope you've had a comfortable week and the girls have been good for you.'

What business is it of hers how they've behaved? She's not their stepmother yet. But she behaves as if she is. Quite bossy, in fact. Penelope doesn't want me to go, and clings to me.

Kate steps forward and takes her hand, pulls her towards her. 'Come now, Penelope. Let your mother go. She'll be back on Monday.'

Penelope begins to cry, and Kate says, 'Now, that's enough. You're lucky your mother's here to visit. She's come a long way to see you.'

Robert walks in with their bags, puts them down and picks Penelope up. 'Come on, pumpkin. We've got some fun things planned for the weekend.' He hands her to Kate and turns to us. 'I'll drive you over there. Bring the bus timetable with you, as you'll need to get a bus back on Monday morning. I'll show you where the bus stop is.'

As we drive away, I look back at the house. The three of them are standing on the step, waving.

I turn to Robert. 'Where are Kate's children?' He'd told me that she has a girl about Sophia's age and a boy three years older.

'Oh, they're with their father at the weekends.'

Kate's house is smaller and more compact than Robert's, furnished with modern furniture and bright-coloured curtains. She's left the fridge stocked for us, and I reheat some pizzas for tea. After we've eaten, Mum goes to bed, and I drift around the living room, looking at the books and record collection. I want to find out who she is, this woman who seems likely to take my place in the family. I read snatches of letters from her English mother, which I find in a drawer of the sideboard; long letters full of complaints and bitching about family members and acquaintances. I sip port from her decanter, replacing it with water so she won't guess. The childhood sneak in me comes out; the child that stole chocolate from the mantelpiece in the living room when my parents weren't there, that rifled through my mother's wardrobe to find the Christmas presents she hadn't wrapped yet. I want to steal something from Kate, to take away some of her power.

Mum doesn't seem to mind moving between Robert's house and Kate's house. Though she is in her late seventies, she doesn't complain on Monday morning when we have to stand on the freezing sidewalk, stamping our feet to keep warm while we wait for the bus, turning our heads away from the icy wind that lashes our exposed flesh and slices through our clothes.

When we get on the bus, she turns to me. 'I've been thinking, Anna.' She pauses.

'Yes, Mum?' I sense a lecture is coming.

'I think you should make more of an effort to be nice to Robert. It is his house, after all, and he's doing his best to make us welcome. Of course, I don't condone what he has done to you and the girls. He had no right to take them so far away from you. But he is a good father, and he is doing his best to make a family life for them here.'

I have no answer to this. When I have to talk to Robert, empty words fall off my lips. I cannot be nice to this man who has taken my life away. Mum and Robert are alike in their respect for reason and social conventions, their fear of emotion. What he has done is not reasonable or moral, but he uses reason to justify his actions on moral grounds.

One morning, he phones and says he'd like to come over and eat with us in the evening.

I hold my hand over the phone and tell Mum.

She says, 'Of course,' and goes to the freezer. She pulls out a beef rump. 'I'll do a roast.'

Over dinner, Robert questions the girls about their day, and tells them the plans for the coming weekend…a visit to Denver zoo with Kate's kids. 'Now, girls, I want to talk to your mother. Go and get ready for bed and I'll come in and kiss you before I go.'

When they've gone downstairs, he asks me to come to his study for a chat. He pours himself a brandy and leads the way. Gesturing towards the chair facing his desk, he sits in his office chair, clears his throat, and frowns down at the desk. 'What are your plans? How do you intend to earn a living?'

'Ah, I've got a Commonwealth scholarship for a coursework MA. Another year to go.'

'You have a good mind. I hope you'll finish your MA this time. Maybe you could get a job in the US once you have a higher degree. Then you could see the girls more often.'

'Oh…I don't know. I've had some problems with my supervisor. It's not going well, and I don't know if I'll be able to finish.'

'I'm sure you can if you put your mind to it. If you set yourself a goal, you can achieve it.'

'Robert do you think you will come back to Australia? Can you get a position at an Australian university?'

'Maybe. But I've got to prove myself here first. I have to provide for my children's future. I'm building a career as a leader in my field. That takes time and hard work. I'm not interested in a hack position at some second-rate university.'

'But Robert…it's not enough for them to see their mother just once a year! They're so young!'

'You should have considered that before you started carrying on like the town bike!' His eyes are narrow, his upper lip stretched across his small white teeth.

We're back on old ground.

I stand up and push the chair in. 'Well, Robert, I'm sorry for what happened, but I can't change it. I don't want my children to live on the other side of the world, and I never wanted to be separated from them.'

He snorts and drains his brandy. 'You're lucky that I'm allowing you access to them, paying your fare, letting you live in my house. Don't push me.'

I retreat to the kitchen. Mum has read the girls a story and gone to her own room. I stack the dishes to be washed in the morning. I hear Robert's footsteps descending the stairs. I take a glass of wine to bed and listen for the sound of the door closing as he leaves to go to Kate's place.

*

Mum's survival kit consists of back copies of English newspapers like *The Observer* and *The Guardian*, a couple of books about classical Greece and Rome and the latest volume of Joseph Campbell on ancient mythology. After dinner, when the children are in bed and the washing up is done, she retires to bed and reads, and talks to me in the morning about what she has read. Her days are spent helping me with a few household chores, going on occasional shopping outings with me, reading and, when the children are home, reading to them and helping them with their homework.

I can't lose myself like she does in books. I try to read, but nothing holds my attention. I play with the idea of transferring to finish my

Masters degree at the city's university, and am granted reading rights in the university library. At the weekend, when the girls are with Robert and Kate, I go and sit in the stacks, reading articles and books on the pastoral poetry of Andrew Marvell, a world and several centuries away. Reading his lovely poem 'The Garden', I am drawn into that world, and long for the transcendence that the poet describes, where the mind creates 'Far other worlds, and other Seas;/Annihilating all that's made/To a green Thought in a green Shade.'

Closing the book, I am back in this winter world. I have a corner desk with a small window that looks out on the mountains. The cold, hard steel of the desk and the chair and the anonymity of this grey corner comfort me strangely. I look out at the icy mountains, glimpsed through smeared glass panes, a wild and unknown world. I cannot live here, I would get lost, more lost than I am in Sydney.

I feel as though I'm acting a part. I'm shocked to find that I can't feel much. My daughters don't feel fully real to me, and I don't feel real to myself. I talk with them, play games with them, read to them, cuddle them, but my heart feels shrunken. I am afraid of loving them too much, of them loving me too much, of having to separate from them again, of being spied on by their father and his girlfriend. I am like a prisoner under surveillance. I have a certain licence, but it is very limited. I am in a foreign country with a ruler who will punish me if I break his laws. I count the days until I can leave.

Twenty-nine

An American friend in Sydney who comes from Colorado has asked me to contact a friend of hers. 'He's a sweet guy. Interesting, too. I reckon you'll get on well.'

I phone Bob and arrange to meet him at a tavern. I recognise him from the photo my friend gave me. He is nice-looking – ruddy cheeks, hazel eyes, curly brown beard and moustache, and a hooked nose. And he is friendly.

He tells me he's an atmospheric scientist.

'What is atmospheric science?' I ask, as we sip bourbon and Coke.

'It's the study of the layers of gas that surround the earth, other planets and moons, and how they interact with the oceans and freshwater systems…all that jazz.' He pulls out a tobacco pouch and some papers. 'Wanna rollie?'

I haven't smoked since last time Danny and I were together. Danny smokes tailor-mades; my Dad used to roll his own.

'Yes, please!'

I watch him deftly roll two perfect little cylinders. Then he leans over and casually strikes the match on the side of his boot. I have never seen anyone do this before, not even my Dad.

After another drink, he leans back on the seat and says, 'Say, wouldya like to go cross-country skiing with me? It's easier than downhill, and there's lots of lovely forests to ski through up the mountains. Only costs four bucks a day to hire the skis.'

'I've never skied in my life. But I'll have a go. Can we do it on Saturday, 'cause I won't be with the girls then?'

We set off in his ute and drive up one of the canyons. When we reach an area that is fairly flat, we head for the fir trees following a trail.

I keep falling over, and he laughs at me and helps me up. After an hour or so, I start to fall forwards instead of backwards on my bum.

'Hey, y're makin' progress!' he calls back over his shoulder, leaning on his skis while I scramble up again.

Around us the fir trees stand, their stiff shapes iced with glossy snow. It is calm and still, and my breath and the swish of my skis on the snow are loud. When I fall, the sound reverberates through the listening forest.

We go for miles, resting every now and then when we find a boulder to sit on.

He has a little pocket camera and takes a photo of me. 'Dynamite!' he exclaims, as he holds it up to frame me.

'What do you mean?'

'Your image, with y'r purple jumper and ski pants and y'r magenta hat, explodes against the white snow. I wish you could see y'rself.'

I've been feeling self-conscious and clumsy all morning, but that dissolves with his words. Perhaps we can be friends, lovers. Perhaps it will last, perhaps I can live here, maybe with him, and study, and see the girls more than once a year.

*

I get a letter from Danny, to my surprise. He tells me a little news of the city and his life, and says he misses me. He signs it 'My love, Danny.' That's the first time he's used that word to me. He even phones me one night, when it's late. Somehow, though I know nothing has changed with him, I feel that he is pulling me back to Sydney. He would never say that; indeed, he's encouraged me to try for a transfer to the university here.

'If you have access to your girls, Petal, it might be easier for you to finish your thesis. You never know, you might become an expat!' But I hear a wistful note in his voice.

I miss him too. But I know he's not the answer. He can't give me a life. I have to find one for myself. My head tells me that I should try to find a way of living near the girls. But, even if I could get a place at uni here, and some sort of stipend or scholarship, or maybe some teaching, I'd have to find somewhere to live, and I'd always be dancing to Robert's tune – his terms for access, his career ruling his decisions about where he'll live. He might decide to take another position in a couple of years' time and I'd have to move again. I know that Bob isn't a long-term prospect. We like each other, we get on well, but I don't feel deeply drawn to him like I do to Danny. As for Danny, I've just about given up hope he'll be more available than he is now. I'll only ever be an escape for him.

To be honest, I don't really know what I want. I want to be able to have my girls back, and I know I can't have that, not while Robert is alive. So long as he's around, since that fatal day when we separated, he has control and will make sure I am only on the fringe of their lives. I can't have them back, so it seems like my choices are to hang around on the wings, seeing them when I can, or create a life for myself and hope that I can see as much of them as he'll allow. I used to think that finding a man who would love me for myself and share himself with me would bring me happiness. Happiness doesn't seem possible any more, now I have lost the girls. When I try to imagine my life in three years' time, or five, my mind goes blank. The truth is, I don't know how to live on my own without them.

My children. I want the unquestioning bond that I had with them before they were taken from me, the certainty of knowing that we were a circle of love, unbroken. I want to relive their childhood with them, to have a second chance to give them the unconditional love that I had lost in my childhood.

I want the impossible.

Thirty

The last day comes. Mum has said her goodbyes and leaves me alone with the children for our last hour together.

Penelope sits on my knee, holding Happy Face, the cloth doll I gave her in Australia before we were separated. Caitlin leans against me, my arm round her.

Sophia does headstands, her tight-clad winter legs poised trembling above her slender body, her skirt half-veiling her long fair hair and tear-wet face. My beautiful upside-down daughter in upside-down land. 'It helps stop the tears,' she says in an upside-down voice.

I want to make this last time with them a happy one. So I sing little songs of Pooh Bear with them and tell them a story. But I can only think of a sad one, which has a half-happy ending.

Demeter had a daughter by Zeus, the ruler of heaven. Her beautiful white-armed daughter was named Persephone. Persephone played with the other goddesses on Mount Aetna in Sicily, where all the flowers of mountain, wood and field grew.

One day, Persephone saw a narcissus, sister of the daffodil. It was shining like yellow gold and had a sweet, delicate perfume. Persephone bent over and plucked it, but when she did, a hole opened up in the ground, and she fell through. The other goddesses ran to tell Demeter what had happened. Demeter wandered for nine days and nights searching for her lost girl. She neglected her duties as goddess of fertility and fruitfulness and the crops failed and fruit did not form on the trees. She had not taught anyone else the secrets of how to make the earth yield food, and so people got very hungry.

Zeus at last decided he had to do something to save the people and the animals from starving, so he sent a messenger god called Hermes down to the Underworld to fetch Persephone.

Hades, king of the Underworld, loved Persephone and didn't want to lose her. He offered her some pomegranate seeds…beautiful, juicy, sweet, shining like jewels. Persephone couldn't resist them and ate them. She wanted to return to her mother, but she had grown fond of Hades too. She ate the seeds because she loved him and was touched by his gift. She knew he would be very sad if she left.

The seeds were her key to the Underworld and sealed her bond with him. So, after that, she returned to the world above with her mother and spent several months of the year there, and then she spent the remaining months with Hades in the Underworld. In those months, it was winter on earth, and the fruit and crops did not grow. When Persephone rejoined Demeter, spring came again, plants and trees blossomed, fruit formed on the branches, and crops grew strong and ripe.

'Mama, was 'Sephone happy?' Penelope asks.

'Yes, darling, she was, because she had the winter world and the spring and summer world, and she could spend time with Demeter and the other goddesses, and with Hades and his friends.'

'Was there snow in the Underworld?' Caitlin asks.

'Yes, lots of it, and Persephone went skiing and ice skating whenever she wanted to.'

'I'm learning to ski,' Sophia says.

'Me too!' Caitlin jumps up and down.

'I go ice skating with my friend Peter and his Mum,' says Penelope.

There's a knock on the door.

'The cab's here,' Mum calls.

'Well, darlings, it's time to say goodbye. I'll come back. I will always love you, and I'll write to you and send you tapes.'

I blow kisses through the cab window; we turn the corner and they are lost again. I fix my eyes on the mountains casting dark shadows over the painted fields – Earth rainbow seen through frosted eyelids.

Thirty-one

I can't keep doing my MA. When I sit at home with library books spread out in front of me, my mind drifts back to the children in their winter world. It will be nearly a year before I see them again. Nine or ten months stretch before me, empty, before I can visit them in winterland.

Things here are the same as before I went to see them. The little house is comfortable and feels safe, my mother is happily settled back into her life, I visit her once a week for dinner, sometimes I go to David and Jo's wine bottlings, Danny calls in about once a week, I go in to uni most days. But now I feel less hopeful. Having seen the girls in the home that Robert has set up for them, and seeing Kate shifting into gear to move in and become their stepmother, I feel less connected with them than I did before. Before, I had my memories or our life in England and the short time we had together in the beach house. Now, my memories of them are shadowed by Robert's ownership of them, the regime he's set up for them, the looming presence of a stepmother chosen for them, and step-siblings. I met them a couple of times when we were there. The boy is tall and gangly, wears glasses, is bossy with the girls. The girl is plump, shy and reserved. When she was there, Sophia and she went into their own little world.

While seeing my daughters again was still only a possibility, I could imagine it in jewelled colours. Now, anything I can imagine for future reunions on his territory is shaded in grey.

When Danny's here, it's the same as ever. After making love, we sit at the kitchen table and talk about my time away, but I don't tell him about Bob. He asks me again if I want to try and move to Colorado.

'I don't think so. There are so many barriers. Once Robert and I are divorced, I'd have to try for an immigrant visa in my own right. After my experience with the consulate last year, I doubt I can get one. And even if I could, I don't know how I'd earn a living there. I'm going to quit the MA. It's not working out for me. I've got a much better chance of getting a job here than I would have in the States.'

'What about the consul who helped you with the visa? Would he help you again?'

'No, he's moved on. He's gone to Venezuela. He wrote to me when I was in Boulder to tell me the news and wish me well.'

'What sort of job do you think you might look for?' Danny says.

'Well, when I was reading the paper on Saturday, I saw an ad for psychiatric nurses, offering a two-year short course for people with degrees.'

'Mental health, eh. A big change for you, wouldn't it be?'

'I want to work with people, and I like the idea of learning more about mental illness. I don't know, Danny. My own life is so different from how it used to be, I've come to question how people live, what matters to them. So many people are busy earning a living, building careers, raising their family, buying and selling houses, playing sport, travelling. I don't feel part of that any more. I accepted the way of life that Robert and I had. I didn't have to work for it. Now I've lost it, it doesn't matter to me. It was just a frame for being mother to my children, and I've lost that. I need to make a life for myself. Maybe I can find meaning in helping other people.'

He stands up and draws me to him. 'You're very strong. You will make a life for yourself. I've watched you survive a situation that would have broken many.' He kisses me and holds me close. Then, as always, he looks at his watch and says he has to go.

*

The advertisement invites people with a degree to apply for mental health training, a shortened two-year course rather than the normal three-year one. They phone me to arrange an interview. I drive out to

North Ryde Psychiatric Centre, which is a sprawling collection of buildings surrounded by parkland. Two senior nurses interview me, a woman and a man, both in their sixties probably. They explain that the hospital, which opened in 1959, has several specialty units, including acute care, a therapeutic community, a children's unit, a psychogeriatric unit, and a medical and surgical ward.

'So, you see,' the man explains, 'you'll have a varied training, including medical and surgical care, and experience in our state-of-the-art therapeutic community. We're evolving mental health care out of the old custodial institution to a rehabilitative model based on brief hospitalisation and follow-up care in the community.'

After the interview, I'm taken on a tour of some of the units and shown the rooms where the graduate class will be given a month's orientation classes. Then I'll be assigned my first unit and return to 'block' (classes in theory) for a week every three months.

Block is an interesting experience. There are more men than women, and a mix of ages, mostly in their twenties or thirties. We are taught by senior nurses on ethics of care, management of acute psychosis, special needs, administration of drugs, and more, by a psychologist on personality disorders and psychological syndromes, by a psychiatrist on diagnosis, traditional treatments such as shock therapy and sleep therapy, and modern drug treatments, and an occupational therapist, on various work programs and diversional therapies. There's lots of reading to do, from Freud to the radical psychiatrist R.D. Laing, to excerpts from the *Diagnostic and Statistical Manual of Mental Disorders*.

It is a different world, one that makes most of the conventions I've been brought up by seem hollow. In the acute admissions ward that is my first placement, I find women and men who have been raised to be normal, but who, through some misfortune of genetics or of life events, have fallen foul of the Australian dream. Young, old, middle-aged, fat, thin, ugly, attractive, well-educated, average, Australian-born, immigrant – any one of them could be my neighbour, my friend, a member of my family. There is nothing exceptional about any of them except that they are here, cast up on the shores of madness and neurosis. Lost. As am I. Yet there is a fine line between us, one that puts me here as a nurse, a therapist, a custodian of their lives, and them as my patients. It was my rupture with the middle-class dream that's brought me here, on the other side of the line from them.

After my first week of orientation, I am told to keep close observation on a woman who is being specialled in a single room. I read in her file that she is acutely psychotic, not aggressive, but hearing voices giving her conflicting messages. She's been sedated but is still hallucinating. Close obs, as it's called, is the only way we have, apart from the tranquillisers prescribed by the registrar, of containing someone who is disturbed in a newish hospital where there are no locked doors.

My patient is lying on the narrow bed, staring at the bare white ceiling, her eyes flicking from side to side. The drug has stopped her restless pacing and explosive utterances but has not stilled her troubled mind. Every now and then, she turns her head, frowning in concentration, as if she is listening to someone, then closes her eyes tight and turns her head away, or shakes her head in silent argument.

I ask her what she is watching, who she is listening to.

'God, of course.' She points to her right-hand side. 'He's saying I've sinned and I need to repent.' She jerks her head to the left-hand side. 'And the devil! He's saying I'm damned and I should end it all.'

'But Eva,' I say, reaching for her hand, 'you know they're not real. I can't see or hear them. You're not well, that's why you're imagining them.'

She turns her head and looks at me, her eyes locking with mine. 'What the fuck do you know? Because you can't see them doesn't mean they're not there.'

I can think of nothing to say. For all my troubles, I've never been psychotic. I don't know what it's like. I've wanted to die, but not because someone is telling me to kill myself. It's another world I haven't entered. She's in it and I'm outside it.

'Sorry, Eva. You're right. I don't know what you're seeing or hearing. Do you want to tell me about it?'

For the next couple of hours, she talks to me about her struggle with God and the devil, her desire to die, her rage at the torment they are putting her through. 'I wish they'd both fuck off, leave me alone, let me live! I want to be normal again, be a mum to my kids, have some fun! It's not fair – why did they choose me?'

Thirty-two

I get up in the morning to go to an early shift at the psych hospital and notice two red lumps on my right leg. I cut myself shaving a couple of days ago. Yesterday, I noticed a red streak near my ankle. After a busy shift, I go to the staff doctor.

His examination is perfunctory. 'Hmm. Infection. I'll give you an antibiotic.' He scribbles a script for a sulfur drug.

I take a dose in the evening. When I wake in the morning, my legs and torso are covered in a red, itchy rash, and the lumps are looking angrier, with smaller ones erupting. I go back to the doctor.

'Hmmm. It's a reaction to the antibiotic. I'll give you an antihistamine and a new script for penicillin. I'll give you an injection now.'

When I get home, I take off my pantyhose and examine my legs. The lumps have spread. Under the rash, many swellings, some no bigger than a small coin, some as large as a hen's egg, are pushing their way to the surface, strange subterranean growths, foci of heat and pain. Alarmed, I go to my GP in Balmain.

After she's examined me thoroughly, she sits facing me, looking concerned. 'I'd like you to have some tests, Anna. Under the allergic reaction, I think you have an auto-immune disorder, but I don't know why you have it. There may be some underlying illness that's causing it. I'll write some forms for you, and I want you to take them to your nearest pathology clinic first thing in the morning. You must fast from midnight.'

I go home and crawl into bed after a couple of glasses of wine.

In the early morning, I wake, needing to pee. I roll out of bed, but when I try to stand, my legs fold under me, crippled by hot waves of pain shooting up them. I crawl into the kitchen and down the garden path to the outside toilet. Once I get back, I collapse into bed, wondering whether to ring an ambulance. No, I can make it to the morning, and then I'll get help.

When it gets light, I crawl again to the toilet. Back in bed, I wait till the clock shows eight, and phone my sister-in-law. She tells me she'll be over in three-quarters of an hour. Then I ring the GP, who tells me to go to the Rachel Forster Women's Hospital in Redfern, where a specialist physician will find a bed for me.

It is excruciating to put weight on my legs and to walk. When I was lying down, my legs felt stiff, heavy and hot. When I stand up and put weight on them, the pain shoots up again, making me cry out.

Jo supports my weight and helps me to pull on undies and a dress. I tell her where to find the things I need to take with me, and she puts them in a carry bag she's brought with her. She locks the back door and helps me hobble out to the car, which she's parked as close as possible to the house. In daylight hours, it is possible to do what was impossible at night.

When we reach the hospital, an orderly comes out with a wheelchair and takes me to admissions. It is a relief to let people I don't know look after me, to give up the effort to care for myself.

*

My flesh is hot, my legs swollen, skin stretched tight like a mummy's, covered in strange hieroglyphics I cannot read. My body resembles an outback landscape, red dirt stripped bare, swollen with anthills, some big, some small.

I lie on a hard, crackly mattress in a hospital bed. The physician under whose name my GP arranged my admission has found me a bed in intensive care, not because I am critically ill, but because there are no other beds available in the hospital. He hasn't seen me yet; the nurse tells me he'll come in to see me on his morning rounds in an hour or two.

He comes at last.

'Hello, Mrs Anderson. I'm Dr Jacobs, a specialist physician. Your GP has described your symptoms to me. We think they indicate an auto-immune disorder called erythema nodosum.'

'What is it? Is it serious?'

'Not in itself. It's an inflammatory disorder of the fatty layer under the skin. It can be triggered by a range of things, and we need to do some tests to find out what the course is. You will get better, but it may take two or three weeks of bed rest.'

I gaze up at his handsome face. So young, so healthy.

'We'll keep you here until a bed becomes available in the medical ward, which may not be till tomorrow. I've prescribed aspirin, which you'll take every four hours, and something to help you sleep tonight. Rest well, and I'll see you again tomorrow.'

The day drags by, and I manage to doze for an hour or two in the afternoon. There was only one other patient in here when I was admitted, but by night-time, all the beds are occupied. It's a semicircular room like a theatre, with a raised dais where nursing staff sit. Their stage is surrounded by beds, all exposed to the light, connected by wires and hoses to an array of machinery. Fever-tossed, it seems to me a creation scene. Nurses are minor deities, ministering to the contraptions of flesh and bone entrusted to their care, bending over them with hushed voices, breathing into tired lungs, seeking to restore life.

From time to time, measured and purposeful activity becomes controlled panic. One patient near me begins haemorrhaging, and within seconds doctors and nurses are working urgently to stop the flow. Pressure bandages, blood transfusions, drips – all fail, and she is rushed off to theatre. A woman opposite me has a head injury; I heard a nurse say she has pressure on the brain. She keeps having seizures, and halfway through the night they start to prepare her for theatre. Suddenly there is a hush, the bustle ceases, and I see them draw a sheet up over her face and pull the curtains around her bed. I doze off for a few minutes. When I look again, her bed is empty. A nurse is cleaning it.

After breakfast, which I eat little of, just a piece of toast and a cup of tea, the nursing staff transfer me to the medical ward. Where earlier I was surrounded by activity and concern, now I am isolated in a small room, bare of furniture except for a bed, a locker and a chair. The walls and ceiling are sterile white, the floor is dull green linoleum, patterned with rusty-red patches…rather like the paddocks at home after the salt-bush seeds took root, born by the giant dust storms of the forties. Fitful sleep comes at last.

The nurse comes in to take my temperature and pulse. Though it is broad daylight outside, she turns on the light. It makes my eyes ache. There is a small strip-light above my bed. There is just one small window facing the street, but from my bed, I can only see a patch of blue sky and some ragged, straggling branches of a tree. Leaves hang motionless; I can't tell what sort of tree it is. The nurse bustles out. I am opposite the nurses' station, so I can hear staff hurrying in and out, answering the phone, calling out to each other, laughing, but I can't make out their words.

Last night, I felt like an impostor in ICU; now I am a prisoner in solitary confinement. I can hear the roar of traffic – trucks, buses, cars, motor-bikes – all sweeping past in waves of hurry and purpose. My room is a pool of quiet, marooned by the ebb and flow of movement and noise. Here, if I close my eyes and blot out the outside world, there are only the crackles of the plastic mattress cover when I move and my breathing. If I lie still and focus on my breath, maybe I can enter the silence and escape.

*

I wake at first light to a dull throbbing in my legs; they are heavy and unresponsive when I turn over to ease the pain in my back and hip.

The lumps are spreading. At first, they were just on my legs, then some came up on my arms. This morning there are a couple on my stomach. I'm not usually aware of how my body feels. I take for granted that it works. Now it is taking over. Getting its revenge. I try lying still on my left side facing the window, with a pillow between my legs. The pillow under my head is too fat, but if I put it slantwise supporting my neck, it isn't too bad.

Before breakfast, a technician comes in and draws several tubes of blood for tests. Later, I'm wheeled off for X-rays: abdomen and chest.

Next day, the doctor comes in to see me, smelling faintly of spice and pine. After greeting me and asking how I feel, he checks my chart. 'You'll be glad to know all your tests have come back normal, except for a raised sedimentation rate in your blood.'

'So why have I got this?'

'Well, since there's no physiological reason we can find, the only conclusion is that it's caused by stress. Have you had a lot of stress in your life lately?'

I meet his eyes, dark and empathic, and look away, afraid I'll start to cry. I haven't cried since we said goodbye to the children. 'Yes, there has.'

'You see,' he says gently, 'the disorder of your blood, manifested in lumps, pain and fever, can only be in response to severe and unrelenting stress. It has built up in your body chemistry to the point where the body starts to attack itself. And although it's a physical disorder, once it's gone, the stress will still be there, and the inflammation may recur.'

'What can I do to stop it recurring?'

'For something like this, there is no long-term treatment. We can only treat the symptoms. For a start, it might help if you tell me a little about what's been troubling you.'

'Thank you, but I don't feel ready to do that.'

'Very well. But I do recommend that, when you are discharged and feeling well enough to go out, you see someone professional who can help you deal with the stress.'

'Thanks, doctor. I will.'

I don't want to see another counsellor. There's no one who can change what's happened. I just have to get used to the way things are and make a life for myself.

*

On the third day, I have a visitor. I wake from an afternoon sleep, troubled by a dream of a child crying in a room that is locked. In the dream, I open the drawer of my hospital locker, my fingers riffling through the contents, searching for a key.

'Anna. Don't cry, dear.' It is my mother, standing beside my bed looking worried. 'What is it?'

'Oh, it was a bad dream.'

Mum is wearing a new navy silk dress she's made, in a graceful style with a crossover bodice and a tie at the waist. Her hat is navy too, with a wide shady brim, a little veil, and a black silk ribbon folded round the crown. Veiled and swathed in the colour of the late evening sky, she looks youthful again.

I pull myself up the bed, and Mum reaches behind me to place the pillows so they support me. It still hurts to move. Mum hands me a thick envelope, airmail, with the name of a legal firm in the top left-hand corner. I look at it reluctantly, with a tight feeling in my stomach.

'It's a letter from Robert's lawyers.'

'Aren't you going to open it?'

'I'll open it later, Mum. I don't feel up to it now. It's just a legal letter. It can't be good news.'

'Do you know yet when your next visit to the children will be?'

'Not exactly, but he did say I could have a month with them next Christmas. That's probably what the letter's about. Or it might be the divorce papers.'

'I wonder how they're getting on?' Mum settles back on the chair, twisting her fingers tightly round the catch on her handbag.

'I don't know. Robert sent me some photos of them a while ago, and a couple of pictures they've done.'

'Has he said anything about coming back to live in Australia? I don't understand why he had to take them to another country.'

I move restlessly in the narrow bed, wishing I could make some excuse and leave the room. 'He says he had to put his career first. I think he wanted to get them as far away from me as possible.'

'Why would he want that?'

'Because he was afraid I'd fight to get them back.'

'And would you have?'

'I don't know if I would've. I don't know.' What I don't say is that I gave in to him because I knew if I tried to take them from him, he would use all the ammunition he had to destroy me (which he has done anyway), and I didn't want them to be torn apart by the battle. On top of that, I felt guilty that I had followed my desire for escape, for love, not thinking of the consequences to them. I was so used to being their main parent and him being the absentee that it hadn't occurred to me he would take them from me. How naive I was.

My eyes are stinging, and there is a lump in my throat that feels bigger than the biggest one on my legs.

'Well, Anna, what's done is done. But I believe they'll come back to you one day.'

I turn on my side, facing Mum, my chin tucked in, my head down. Mum's feet are crossed at the ankles. Her shoes are bumpy and worn. She told me that she had a severe vitamin B deficiency after I was born and couldn't breastfeed me. She was forty-five, they'd been through years of drought and the Great Depression, and their diet was poor. She had to feed me on Sunshine dried milk, though she'd breastfed all the others. She couldn't wear shoes for a year and had to walk on the sides of her feet, the soles were so painful. She wore an old pair of slippers around the house but wouldn't go into town or anywhere away from home. She cured herself by grinding flour and baking bread from the wheat Dad grew in the home paddock, after he'd installed irrigation ditches and a pump. But ever since then, her feet have been so deformed that any new pair of shoes has to be worn in gradually until the leather stretches and softens.

I lift my head so I can see her face. 'Mum, you know how you used to tell me you have second sight?'

'Ye-es?' She opens her bag and ferrets through its contents.

'Well…can you see what will happen? Will they come back to me?'

She takes out her compact, powders her cheeks and nose, and gazes in the mirror. 'I can't foretell the future. I just have a strong feeling, that's all...that you haven't lost them.'

'Thank you, Mum.'

We make a little more conversation, then Mum checks her watch.

'I'd better go, if I'm to catch the next ferry.' She pulls her gloves on and bends over to kiss my flushed face.

At least she hasn't changed her perfume, I smile to myself.

Mum tells me they are not lost, they will come back to me. So I must make that leap of faith, trusting that we will find each other again and not be separated by thousands of miles. Even if we cannot live together, I vow to hold onto my love for them and theirs for me, to let them know that I love them, have always loved them, will always love them, and that one day, we will be together again. I have to hold onto that hope and help them to hold onto it. Without hope, I will die.

My head aches, my whole body hurts.

My eyes fall on the chair where Mum sat an hour or so ago. I wish I could sleep. The night air of the street drifts in my open window. It is heavy with the scent of jasmine, mixed with decaying rubbish and traffic fumes. Inner-city air, a potpourri of the clutter, the bustle and the waste products of people's lives, sweetened by flowers of tenacious shrubs and vines that cling to pockets of earth in courtyards and footpaths.

*

My mother and other family members have visited me. But not Danny. I wrote and told him I was in hospital, but I've heard nothing. I keep hoping he'll come and see me, or at least send a card or some flowers. Since I started psychiatric nursing, I haven't seen so much of him because of my shift work, but he still phones me every few days, and comes to see me when he can. He's never said he loves me or made any sort of commitment. A few months ago, he started a practice of getting me to go with him on his drive home from my place in Balmain to the North Shore suburb where he lives. He'd pay for a taxi to take me home.

I'd sit beside him, as close as I could get, and let my fingers play on the back of his neck, stroking that tender spot below his hair line. When we reached the main road of his suburb, he'd pull in near the taxi rank and we'd hold each other and kiss deep and tender, without words. I'd get out and stand at the taxi rank, and he'd wait to make sure I got a cab.

This is all I have, these remnants, shreds of memory. All he can spare.

The phone rings in the nurses' station opposite my room. My body tenses. I lie waiting for the nurse to come in and tell me he's phoned, sending his love. She doesn't come.

At least, I think, as I turn restlessly in the bed, I'm getting my body back. For a while, it was alien to me, a war zone, colonised by pain and fever. My smooth flesh, which I have always taken for granted, became deformed, unrecognisable, the site of a battle in my bloodstream over which I have no control. But why this way, I wonder? Why am I unable to walk, to look after myself? What does this mean about the way I've been living my life? Why did it not happen after I first lost the children? Why now, two years later? What can I do to change my life so that it is liveable? How can I become well enough to go on, to begin again? The doctor says the illness could return if I am under extreme stress again in my life. How can I avoid that? What future have I without my children, without Danny, just on my own, with nothing to look forward to except surviving from one day to the next?

I think back again to my lost childhood and remember how Mum struggled to carry on after Dad left, how she kept the property going for years, most of the time with only me to help her, and in the end, after she sent me away to boarding school, on her own. Until Dad returned and threw her out. How did she do it? At the time, I saw only my own pain and loneliness, and felt constrained to support her, without compassion for her situation. I felt a prisoner and resented the loss of freedom and my father's love, the responsibility, the unending hard work. I blamed Mum for Dad's abandonment of us. Now, I know how hard it was for her, how lonely she was, despairing at times when the work was too hard, when the rains didn't come, when the endless summer raged on, when Dad took all the profits, when the allowance he paid was never enough to pay the bills. My mother's courage and determination were astonishing, and I feel that I can never live up to her example. Certainly, she would never have abandoned her children the way I did.

How different my own losses are. My children – my children – my children. The years with Robert were lived by another woman. I can't relate to her. The only connection I have with her is the children, and they are lost to me. I left myself as wife and mother, walked away, unable to live that life any more. I can't look back, like Mum perhaps did, and reflect that I've done everything I can to save my way of life, my home, my family. Where Mum tried to preserve, I destroyed. Mum put what she saw as her children's needs first, sacrificing her own needs for company, love, intellectual stimulation, to stay on at Arendal. Yet she didn't regret it. What she did regret was having left it precipitately, not having stood her ground when Dad returned. She gave in to his assertion of ownership. Maybe we aren't so different. For Mum, Arendal was at stake. For me, it was my children. We both lost to a man we built our lives around, who kept the power of ownership and property. Robert regards our children as his property. He loves them, but his love is based on possession. Mine is defined by loss.

Mum is supportive but still doesn't understand why I left. To her, no sacrifice is too great to keep the family together. A woman's place is with her husband and children, and it isn't as if I had a bad husband. Robert was a good provider, a loving father, a successful academic, building an international reputation. My children are young and need me. I disgraced myself and my family by leaving. I followed in my father's footsteps. He was a deserting husband and abandoning father. I am, as Robert told me in that phone call from America, 'a deserting wife and abandoning mother'.

She is my lifeline now. She might judge me, but she hasn't deserted me, and she will do anything she can to help me, to support me, to uphold my right and my children's right to see each other.

My fever has gone, but the lumps on my legs are still red and angry. I am sick of lying here, turning from side to side, staring at the floor and the bare walls. To keep my thoughts from the children, from that black hole that is their lives without me, my life without them, I let my mind drift back again to childhood.

*

The doctor steps into my room and smiles to see me sitting up in bed. 'You're looking better, some colour in your cheeks, and that unnatural flush has gone.' He sits down by my bed. 'Well, Anna, you're well enough to go home at the end of the week. But you're not well enough to go back to work yet. You must go to your mother's house to convalesce for a couple of weeks. All the repeat tests have come back normal, but there's still a raised sedimentation rate in your blood. You'll need to come and see me at my rooms once a month and keep having blood tests for at least six months.'

'Oh…OK. Thanks for looking after me.'

'Here's the name of a counsellor I can recommend, when you're ready. Take care of yourself.' He hands me two cards, one for his Macquarie Street practice, one for a psychologist.

I am at the edge of the world, lost even to the broken half of it that I knew. I am outside it in a neutral time and space that has no known horizons. When I am released from this hospital bed, I'll have to try and find a shape to my life again. The effort seems too great. I wanted to be seriously ill, so that I could die without having to make a decision.

Only the past has meaning. The future is blank. I am disappointed that the lumps are fading, and I am getting better. It means I'll have to face life again. I've grown attached to the lumps – they made me an interesting case. I throw the psych's card in the waste-paper bin after the doctor leaves the room.

Danny… Perhaps he is the man Freud said I should have married; the one who resembles my father, in his private self, though not in his public, which is closer to my mother's model of a good man. With me, he is loving, kind, accepting, playful, delighting and delightful. Away from me, he is the Law, the City, Commerce, upholding and serving the world of middle-class business and morality – all of which my father, in his small rebellion, his desire to escape the web of duty and desire, flouted. And which I have escaped from, at terrible cost.

Danny gives me himself, but only in small doses, at times that suit him. He uses me as an emotional and erotic escape from the duties and obligations of his life, while giving me all the emotional and legal support he can to help me survive the fracture in my life. We are each other's boltholes, but I want the whole man, and he does not want the whole me. I still dream of a day when he might leave his wife, but he holds fast to the web of his family and social position. I want to love him openly, though he's never given any hint that this might be possible. I don't want to live in his leafy suburb or walk the grey tunnels of the city with him or mix with all his city friends and associates. I want him to have another life with me that is separate from the suburb and the city but is not hidden or wrong. I want to be able to tell my friends and family that he is my lover, not to have to keep him a secret. I want to be seen with him, and for him to name me to others and feel proud of being seen with me.

I've been waiting all my life for a man to come along and rescue me. Ever since my father left, I've had a romantic idea of love as a transforming power that will make my life meaningful and happy.

Dad was my first love, David my brother was my second, but Dad left, and David went away to university. I used to wonder what my life would've been like if Dad had stayed. Perhaps the shine would've worn off as I got older.

When I am strong enough, I'll return to my psych nursing job. At least that isn't a disaster. It is the only part of my life I look forward to resuming. It is fascinating working with people whose lives seem more broken and messy than mine. When I started working there, I thought:

why are they mad, depressed, suicidal, and I'm not? I could so easily be in their position. There but for the grace of God go I.

Now, I think the line between me and them is so thin, I've stepped over it. Will I ever have a normal life? I cannot imagine it. How can I make a life for myself, as a single woman without my children?

*

The day before my discharge, the doctor visits me. He is perfectly groomed as usual, gleaming with health and energy. I feel old, pale, flabby and tired. My body has lost the unnatural flush it had when the lumps were there and is an unhealthy pasty white. I smell stale and sickly. My hair hasn't been washed for over two weeks. It is itchy and oily.

'Well, Anna, you're leaving us tomorrow. Don't expect too much of yourself at first. You'll need to increase your daily activity very slowly, rest often. You can get up today and have a shower, but you'll need to have a nurse with you.'

'Thanks, doctor. Thanks for all your care.'

'Come and see me in a month's time. Phone my office on Monday and make an appointment to see me.'

After the nurse has finished her morning round of bed-making and dressings, she comes with a wheelchair and helps me to the shower. As I stand up, waves of fire run through my legs. I cry out and collapse on the bed, surprised by the intensity of the pain. I feel like the little mermaid in Hans Christian Andersen's story, walking on knives so I can be with humans. I have a couple of goes at getting into the chair. The nurse wheels me out of the room.

I am out of prison for the first time since the morning they brought me to this ward; I see the corridor, the nurse's station, the double doors leading to the outside world. The bathroom is at the end of a long corridor. The nurse parks the chair next to the shower cubicle. I pull my nightie off and start to get out of the chair. As soon as I put weight on my legs, the pain shoots up. I collapse back, feeling faint and sick.

'Take it slowly, Anna. There's a shower chair here so you don't have to stand up. Here, I'll take the side off the wheelchair so you can slide over.'

The warm water runs over my body, and I put my head back so it runs through my hair and over my face. I work shampoo through my hair, rubbing my scalp to relieve the itchiness. Then I let it all wash out, over my face and body, till the water runs clear again.

The nurse returns from answering a bell. 'Are you done? Great. Try standing this time but hold onto the rail and take as much weight as you can with your hands.'

I manage to stand for a few moments. The pain is less. For the first time, I feel anxious to walk again, to look after myself. Back in my room, I get out of the wheelchair and walk a few steps to my bed. I practise again a few times, taking short walks around the bed. My legs still hurt, but it is easier than the first time.

Thirty-three

Mum comes and takes me home in a cab to her house. As I walk slowly and painfully down the path and through the kitchen door, I wish I were back in hospital, where I didn't have to put up a front. Maybe that is what this is all about, why I got ill – trying to live the life I've been expected to live, to keep up appearances.

Mum's life is very quiet and regulated and I feel like a child again, finding a certain comfort in a structure that my life has lacked. She gets up every morning at five o'clock, just as she used to in the country. She makes a pot of tea and goes out in her dressing gown to pick up the newspaper from the front lawn. She gets the *Sydney Morning Herald* every day and, once a month, the *Guardian* and the *Observer* from England. She says she doesn't feel she's started her day until she's read the paper right through. It provides her with her main topics of conversation for the day. Morning tea is at ten thirty, lunch at twelve thirty, dinner at seven. At midday and five o'clock, she gets out the bottle of dry sherry and pours us each a glass, served with cracker biscuits and cheese. We have a glass or two of white wine with dinner. Like her cups of tea, it is a habit that gives her pleasure and a modest escape from the monotony of her days, and the knots her mind worries over. She's always been a worrier, and since there is little in her own life to worry about now, she worries about other people's lives, especially mine. I've failed spectacularly to live up to my early academic success and my marriage to a man who promised to have a great career.

My children are a source of joy to Mum, but now they are gone. To do her credit, after her first dismay and shame at my status of 'deserting wife and abandoning mother', she gives me whole-hearted support and continues to maintain that the girls will come back to me eventually.

Early on, she was sympathetic to Robert. They have a lot in common, and he did a good job of painting me as the scarlet woman to Mum and other members of the family. But since he took the children out of the country, she's changed her mind about him.

The days drag almost as much as they did in hospital. I find it hard to make conversation and pretend to be composed and comfortable when I feel so lost and adrift. Emptiness, politeness and boredom are my daily companions. Gradually, my thoughts turn to the future.

*

I arrive home at Mullens Street late one afternoon in time to glimpse my neighbour creeping along the walls of houses that line the street, walking stick in one hand, shopping bag in the other. Her head is bent, concentrating on each uncertain step. She doesn't notice me getting out of the cab.

Buses and trucks roar past, smoky traffic fumes wash over me. The dogs and cats have been busy in my courtyard. I want to clean it out and plant something there. Perhaps a jasmine vine will grow, sweeten the air a bit. The house smells musty, but when I open the windows, a light breeze blows in from the docks, refreshing me with smells of the harbour. After I've unpacked, I sit at the purple table, sipping a glass of David's wine. Above the muffled roar of traffic, I can hear the drunks again, yelling curses at each other. At least they don't pretend. I smile and try to catch their words.

I phone Danny's secretary in the morning, to make an appointment to discuss the divorce papers Robert had his lawyers send me while I was in hospital. I had forwarded them to Danny and asked him to let the American lawyers know I was in hospital and unable to respond to them for a few weeks.

He phones me that night and asks if he can visit me. I say yes, though I have resolved not to go on the way we were.

It is late when I open the door to his brisk knock. He hands me a large bunch of red roses and comes in carrying the usual beer and wine.

It is just like it used to be as we sit and chat. I share his cigarette; he leans back in the old wooden swivel chair. It creaks as he moves.

'Danny, why didn't you come and see me, or at least send a message? I was very ill and unhappy. I was dying to hear from you.'

'Petal, I wanted to, but I've been busy with a big and difficult case. I've not been well either. In fact, I've felt like chucking it all in a few times. But I'm a lot better now for seeing you.' He takes my hand and squeezes it. 'Will you let me hold you again? I've missed you.'

I pour another glass of wine and hesitate. I so want to say yes. I desire him as much as the first time I saw him. I don't believe I'll ever feel like this about anyone else.

He lights another cigarette and tops up his beer. But I remember the lumps, the pain and fever and the loneliness that no one but Mum shared with me. I wrote to him in hospital, but he didn't answer. I remind myself that he is still married, if not to his wife, to the law, to his family, to the city.

'No…' I drain my glass. 'It's over, Danny.'

He looks up, meeting my eyes. His eyes are dark, deep like river pools. I don't want to drown again. I turn my face away and get up, collecting empty glasses and bottles. I stand at the sink. The glassy black of the window reflects back to me a face scarred with grief and loss.

Danny walks over and puts his arms around me from behind, leaning his head on my shoulder.

'Someday, some time, some place, we'll meet and be lovers, freely, without secrecy, won't we?' I say silently, not wanting to accept that this is the end.

He doesn't answer.

After he's gone, I sit at the purple table, finishing my wine, smelling the warm fragrance of frangipani mixed with traffic fumes drifting in on the night breeze.

Postscript

The second visit at the end of 1974 passed quickly. I had less access to the children, as Kate and her children had moved in, and I stayed with Bob, my skiing buddy. He was a gracious and easy-going host, and I was able to have the children visit and stay overnight sometimes. During the week, when Kate was at uni (she was doing a PhD in Social Work) and her kids were at school, I could visit my daughters; Robert had taken them out of school for the last week of term.

I felt like a ghost that materialised at times but kept fading. I had to force myself to enter their world, where I felt excluded, and no matter how they clung to me, wanting me to stay, I knew I had to leave again, and could not return except under the temporary licence of the one who kept me away from them. I struggled to love them, to let my flesh meet theirs, for I knew I would have to tear it apart again.

When I left again, I felt trapped in a story written by a cruel, narcissistic king who had banished me and allowed me to return briefly once a year to his kingdom to see my children.

Towards the end of 1975, Robert brought the girls back to Australia in a blended family with Kate and her two children. He took a position in a university in Melbourne. So they were still far from me, but not as far, and I could now see them twice a year, instead of once.

For many years, I played a part as a holiday mother with no rights beyond two weeks of my daughters' lives twice a year, with no say in how they were brought up, what schooling they had, how they were loved or disciplined or not loved, how they spent their leisure time, what clothes they wore, what shaped their spirits and their emotions. I had a bit part as an extra, the other mother, who came on stage briefly and did my best to bundle my love for them into small parcels, to give them short-dated happiness and a sense of safety and belonging. What I had to give them was everything and nothing. I gave them hope and knowledge of a love that was not bondage, that did not tie them to a life and a family they hadn't chosen; I was the parent who loved and respected them as they were, but I could not be present in their lives. I could not protect them from the blended family in which they were their father's pets and their stepmother's and step-siblings' rivals.

'I'll look after your children for you, Anna,' Kate had said to me when she waved me off at the end of my second visit.

I did not believe her, I did not want her to, but I had no say. I found out, when it was too late to do anything, that her affection for them was unreliable, subject to explosive outbursts of cruelty and discriminatory treatment.

Their father, they told me when they were old enough to voice their pain, had sat down with them when they reached the States, and told them that they could choose which parent they lived with, but if they chose to leave him, he would die. Penelope, not even three, holding onto her fading infant memories of me, wanted to return to me; but Caitlin and Sophia, worried that their father would indeed die if they left him, told her that they would stay, and she should stay with them. He did to them what he did to me: he threatened them with his death. And they believed him, as I had. What choice did they have?

They did not tell me this till they were grown-up.

There was no resolution to this story in their childhood. The arc that moves from point of conflict and an initiating event that drives the story to its climax was not resolved until they were adults. Indeed, it is still resolving, for 'recovery', if there is such a thing, is a lifelong process. Recovery means return to a normal state of health. In this broken family story, there is no normal. Or it means regaining possession or control of something that was lost. There can be no such recovery, for what was lost, the living, loving, everyday relationship of mother and children with each other, was destroyed. The safety, the security, the trust, were gone. The choices their father and I made, separately, and the decisions that were forced on me, destroyed their childhoods. We continued to grow separately but grew broken. The fracture lines are deep in each of us.

It has been more a process of growing through the trauma than recovering from it, for one can never return to how one was. The climax was our first reunion, but it led to more of the same… separation, again and again. We were trapped in a cruel cycle created by their father.

Through all the moves I made, from one house to the next, they visited me, and we had brief, happy times together. These times were always conditional on their father's consent and on the agreement that they would return to him when their holiday was over. There was always the pain of parting again. And behind those holiday times, shadows lay.

I felt like my girls' big sister. Knowing how regimented and bossed around they were at home, I let them do pretty much whatever they liked as long as they were kind to each other. But I was worried about Penelope. By the time she was seven years old, her normal bubbly, happy personality was shadowed by a nervous, twitchy self-consciousness. She talked to herself sometimes and bit her nails. I longed to be her full-time mother again, to be mother to the three of them, to keep them safe, to give them a happy, carefree childhood, the one they deserved, the one I'd dreamed for them.

Each time we had to say goodbye, it was torture. Caitlin would cling to me and sob, Penelope would snuggle in my arms, and Sophia would bury her face in my bosom. When the boarding call came, I would have to take them to the hostess and hug and kiss each of them a last goodbye. The tears were endless, and after they'd gone, I'd go home, drink a couple of glasses of wine and lie in bed until I could cry no more. It felt like a love affair, the longing, the desire to be with my beloveds, the joy when they were there, the nagging concern that they were not happy at home, the grief when we had to part, the loneliness and emptiness when they were gone. The inability to change the way it was, the knowledge that I had no control over how they were being brought up. That it would never be any different.

There were hints, but nothing clear. In the spaces between our times, they wrote to me, and I wrote to them, though I have no copies of my letters. I have kept a bundle of their letters and pictures, but most of them aren't dated and, as with my memories, there are many gaps. They told me of inconsequential things, their outings, the movies they saw, the books they were reading, their school, their activities like Brownies and tennis.

A letter from Caitlin, written to me when I still lived in Sydney, gave me a glimpse of her struggle to live in the blended family. She sounds much older than her eleven years.

Dear Mummy,
Thanks for the stamps, they're really pretty. Sorry I left my jumpers. I remembered them as soon as I arrived home. I've recovered now and look forward to Christmas, so I don't think about my present problems.

...I've taken to gardening, so much I've asked for my own patch in the garden and I'm going to plant flowers in it and weed every day in my garden.

You know as soon as I got your letter, I started to write this one to you. Usually I would just put it aside and wait for a couple of days then force myself to write back! It was hard to admit that to myself when I thought about it, but I guess it's the truth. I find myself trying to leave the family and be alone and independent. It's just pure bliss to be sitting in a park under a tree and the sounds of cars, the city and people far away. Just thinking of nothing in particular and the only sounds are birds singing and trees whispering.

School's fine and I'm happy so, well, I guess that's all.
Lots of love and kisses
Caitlin

In another letter, dated not three weeks after her twelfth birthday, Caitlin told me of their long, boring bus trip back to Melbourne, and said, 'I am really depressed much more than I usually am after leaving you. I have also had a series of headaches.'

That year, 1979, at the end of the year, I was packing to move to

Western Australia. I had struggled for six months over the decision to move. I had met again a man who had been a friend of ours when we were living in England. Michael was Australian too, living there with his family on a long working holiday. Early in 1979 I had a letter from him, saying he would like to see me; he was separated from his wife, living in Perth, and had taken a new job that required him to come to head office in Sydney for an induction.

So we met, had dinner together, and agreed to meet again next day. A weekend in each other's company seemed enough to base the prospect of a life together on. I was thirty-nine, he was forty-eight. We both wanted happiness, a mutual love, a last chance to create our own family. We corresponded for the rest of the year and talked on the phone. I did not want to move to Perth, but he was not willing to consider moving to Sydney and I feared I would lose him if I did not go. For seven years on my own, I had carried the dream of a relationship that would give me something of the love I had lost in childhood, one that was real and would not disappear. I felt that this was the meaning of life, that unless I found this, I could not be happy. I felt such emptiness in my life, behind my work, my friendships, my Sydney family – always I was searching to fill that gap. Often, I wished I could leave the world and come into it again on different terms. My life was so different from how I'd dreamed it.

So I made the decision to go to Perth to be with him. The children visited me for the last time in Sydney, before Christmas.

I was worried about Caitlin. She had lost her young chubbiness. Her hair was no longer flossed red, more of a ginger brown, and her fair skin was freckled. She wasn't happy with her physical body, and she wasn't happy in herself.

She came to me one morning when the other two were with their Nanna, making mince pies for Christmas. She asked me to let her stay with me, not go back to Melbourne.

'Caitlin, why, darling, what's wrong?'

'I hate living there! I hate Kate and her kids. She hates us.'

'Tell me more.' I put my arm around her and tried to slow my breathing, to listen, not to panic.

'She hits us, Penelope and me, when Dad's not around. She doesn't hit Sophia, because Sophia's good and studies hard and isn't messy like me. She's jealous of Penelope because she's Dad's baby, and she gets mad at me 'cause I answer back and I'm messy and I lose things.'

'Tell me about when she hits you.'

Caitlin's face crumpled, and tears slid down her cheeks. 'She hit Penelope across the face last week because she forgot to make her bed. I told her to stop it, and she turned on me and whacked me across my legs with a rolled-up magazine. She whacked me so hard I fell onto the bed.'

She started to sob, and I held her. I was with her in her pain, but my mind was in turmoil. What was I to do? How could I send them back? How could I keep them?

'Darling, tell me why you want me to send Sophia and Penelope back and keep you here. What about Penelope?'

'Mum, if I'm not there, I think she'll be all right. I stick up for her, and that makes Kate worse. And she's Dad's pet, and I think if we all left him, he really would die.'

'Darling, I think we need to have a family talk about this. I want to talk with the three of you about it.'

'No, Mum, please don't tell the others! I don't want them to know yet!'

'Why not?'

''Cause Sophia will try and talk me out of it and Penelope will be upset.'

I brooded on this for a day or two and made an appointment to see Danny. I told him Caitlin's story.

He looked serious and asked me a few questions. He sat back in his chair and looked at his clasped hands for a moment or two. Unclasping them and stretching his fingers out on the desk, he leaned forward. 'Anna, I hate to say this, but you'll have to send her back.'

'Why?' I felt a lump in my throat and a tight band across my forehead. How could I send them back when they were being punished and hit for trivial things?

'Because Robert has custody of them, and you would be breaking the law by keeping them with you. If you want to contest custody and make a case that he and his wife are unfit parents, your children will have to go to court and testify.'

'Oh.' My head throbbed, my throat was bursting. 'I hadn't thought of that. I thought I could keep them with me and make a statement, maybe get them to sign it, an affidavit or something.'

'No.' He paused and drew a deep breath. 'The reality is, he holds the cards. He has possession, he has a good profession and income, a house, and they've been with him for several years. He returned to Australia, he will say, so that you could have access to them.'

I sighed. 'Whereas I have nothing. I'm a nurse on a low income, I rent, I'm single…so far…and he will say I left them in the first place. No matter that his wife loses her temper with them and hits them, no matter that he's away a lot and doesn't know what's going on, or if he does, he does nothing about it!'

'I'm afraid so. Not unless you can make a case for cruelty or neglect and the girls are willing to testify in court. And in the meantime, they will have to return to him.' He lit a cigarette and offered it to me.

I was angry with him, because he represented the law, the male-dominated legal system, the whole fucking unfair system I was up against. Yet I knew he was right. And I did trust him. I knew he wanted to help me, he wanted me to have some happiness, some of what I'd lost, he knew none of this was my fault, he was just telling me how it was.

I went to see my brother David in his office. I told him Caitlin's story.

He said, 'Well, how do you know she's telling the truth? Maybe she wants to live with you and she's making this up. And why would she want to leave her sisters behind?'

I stared at him. 'What the fuck do you know? You don't know what it's like to be her, to have to live with a woman who scolds her and her little sister for trivial things and hits them when she feels like it! Of course she wants to live with me. Penelope would too, if she had a choice. I'm not sure about Sophia.'

'Look, Sis, the reality is he has custody and you don't. Danny's right, they'd have to go to court to testify if you try to get them back. Do you want to put them through that? Would they want to go through it?'

I had no words. I picked up my bag and got up, pushing the chair back, and walked out. Men ruled. Men made the laws, men administered them, men had the power and the money. I was just a woman, a mother who left her children eight years ago, and I couldn't save them from living with a woman who was cruel to them and a father who was absent a lot of the time.

When I told Caitlin the news, she drooped her head and said nothing.

I held her close and said, 'I don't want to send you back, but I have to for now. I want you to tell your father what's been happening. Will you?'

She nodded.

'And when I come down to Melbourne with Michael, I'll talk to him too. I promise.'

Michael was coming over to help me pack up and we were planning to hire a car and drive down to Melbourne and on to Adelaide, then get a plane to Perth.

Caitlin said little. I sensed she had withdrawn into herself, and I couldn't reach her. I was abandoning them all over again, only it was worse because they didn't just have a father who loved them but was often absent, they had a stepmother and step-siblings whom they hadn't chosen, and their father chose to turn a blind eye to the abuse they suffered.

At the airport, as we waited for their plane, Caitlin sat on my knee, sobbing, her face buried in my neck. I had my arms around the other two, and they sat in close, leaning against me. I hadn't told them about Caitlin's request to stay with me, but I think they knew.

'Darlings, I love you forever, to the sky and back. Write to me when you get home. And tell your father I will be coming down soon, and I want to talk to him.'

As I waved goodbye to them, three lonely figures walking behind the hostess along the corridor to the plane, I lost them all over again. Always, it would be like this. Always. I would have to let them go, not knowing what their lives were like without me, only hearing snippets, not having any say in how they lived.

*

Michael and I drove down and stopped at the beach house where they were spending Christmas. It was getting dark when we arrived.

Caitlin ran out to the car and I opened the door.

She hugged me and whispered, 'Mum, don't say anything to Dad. I've talked to him and it's all OK, he's talked to Kate, he says it won't happen again.'

I held her away at arm's length so I could see her eyes. Sapphire blue, with dark rims around the irises. Even now, in the twilight, they shone. 'Darling, I'm glad you have talked to him. But I still want to talk to him myself. I want him to know that I know about Kate.'

When I did talk to him, he said how hard it had been for Kate to take on three young girls, how much she loved them, how good she was to them. That they'd had an honest talk about things, and she had promised it wouldn't happen again. She had been stressed, he'd been away. He'd try to make sure he was at home more.

'Why do I find it hard to believe that? You have the law on your side. But nothing is set in concrete. If there are grounds for changing the custody arrangement, the court will decide. I will be watching, and if I have reason to believe they are not being treated well, I will take action.'

My words felt empty. What could I do from three thousand miles away? He held all the cards and he knew it.

When we left and drove away, I felt I had abandoned them again. I had let Caitlin down. She'd asked me to rescue her and I'd failed her. I felt that this was a pivotal moment in her life, and my failure to help her consigned her to a life where I would not be able to reach her, to keep her safe. I'd done it before, but this time, she had asked for my help and I couldn't give it. She wouldn't trust me again.

With a heavy heart, I drove off with Michael towards my future life. There seemed to be no way I could change the course of their lives, save them from unhappiness. And I was moving further away from them. Till now, Robert had paid their fares when they came to visit me. From now on, I would have to pay for their airfares to Perth, twice a year. Michael had made it clear that he couldn't afford it on his salary, so it was up to me to find a job and pay their expenses.

A small price to pay, but it nearly drove Michael and me apart when I became pregnant with our son, for he insisted that if I couldn't work, we couldn't afford to bring the girls over for a visit. I could not contemplate not being able to see them at all and was on the verge of leaving him before our son was born and going to live in Melbourne to be near them. Our marriage of less than two years nearly split apart. He saved it by taking a job in the Pilbara, much better paid than his Perth one, and we moved up there. Two weeks before our son was born, we moved back to Perth; Michael had been sacked because he refused to do things that were against his professional code of ethics.

Our marriage got off to a rocky start and didn't last more than five years; but I managed to keep seeing the girls throughout their childhood. And when Penelope turned fourteen, she chose to come and live with me; the Family Law Act had changed to allow children of fourteen or more to choose which parent they lived with without having to go to court. By then, Caitlin and Sophia had left their blended family and started their own difficult journeys into adulthood. I could do nothing to change their paths; I could only witness and be there for them whenever I could, and wait for a time when we could live closer to each other and unpick some of the knots that had been tied in our past lives, gently unfold some of the stories we'd not been able to share, and make space for future stories where our love was not barred by the law and by patriarchal privilege.

*

In a strange way, Robert gave me a gift – a cruel one, disguised as a challenge. He forced me to leave my daughters and to be separated from them through their childhood. The challenge was to find my own way in life, to define myself, to stay true to my love for them and to survive. The challenge to my daughters was to survive abandonment and abuse and make their own lives in their own images, not in anyone else's. That has been the making of them as strong, independent, creative, loving women. It's been a lifetime journey for each of us, and we have survived it and stayed true to ourselves and to each other. Whereas his victory was a Pyrrhic one. He thought, in separating us from each other, that he would be able to hold onto his children and to have control over their lives. His possession was tainted by his abuse of power, and his victory turned to defeat. He became old, ill, lonely and bitter, and it was only in the last months of his life that he began to realise the mistakes he had made.

My further challenge has been to forgive him for forcing me to leave my daughters, and for failing to keep them safe and give them the happy childhoods they deserved. It has been a long journey, fraught with pain, remorse, anger and loneliness. Only recently can I say that I've let go of my judgement of Robert. I chanced on a photo of us on our wedding day, outside the entrance to the restaurant where we had our wedding reception – Le Trianon. I am facing the camera side-on, left hand holding my gloves, veil back. He is facing me, head tilted, looking into my face, laughing. I am laughing too, but my gaze is away from him. You would say, if you didn't know our history, 'This man is happy, delighted with his bride. She is delighted with being a bride, but her attention is not on him.'

There is truth in that. I saw him as a holder of my future, someone steady who would create a life for us both. I wasn't in love with him, not as I know love now. I was attracted to his charisma, his intelligence, his seriousness, his sense of purpose, his gaiety when he danced or watched a comedy show, his adventurousness and willingness to take risks. After all, he took a big risk marrying me, a not-quite-grown-up young woman with different values and dreams and a very different way of seeing the world.

I felt he would not abandon me. And he didn't. Not in his terms. He believed that having children would help me settle down, find a purpose in life. He took us to England, he worked hard, he bought a house we could live in happily and safely, he earned enough for us to be able to have a lively social life, to travel and, in the last couple of years, to live in our dream Tudor house in a charming village. He left me and the children again and again when he went on conferences, when he went to work after hours and at weekends, when he fell in love with some other woman in a faraway place, but he always came back, and I don't think he considered leaving me, because I was our children's keeper and carer. He swore he would do nothing to break up the family.

I abandoned him because I felt I had become his prisoner. I see now that he loved me in the best way he could, holding a stranger, someone he really didn't know or understand, trying to keep her safe and to make her happy.

But I felt trapped. I wanted to be free to express myself and create my own life, and I hadn't learned how to do that. I mistakenly identified happiness with being in an equal, loving relationship, where we could be ourselves and recognise each other and leave each other to be free. I thought I'd found that when our neighbour knocked on our door. But he was as unrealistic and impulsive as I was, and he was not able to rescue me or himself from the domestic castles we were imprisoned in.

I forgive Robert for loving me in the way I didn't want to be loved and I forgive myself for not loving him in the way he wanted to be loved and for leaving him in a way that damaged him, damaged my children, and damaged me. Out of that damage, beauty has grown, and strength, and courage to go on living and loving, even through separation and absence. It has been a very hard lesson to learn, one that he and I have imposed on our children. They had to learn to endure separation and loss and living with people who were not kind or safe a lot of the time, with parents who were not there when they needed them. They were very wounded when they became adults, but they have turned those wounds into crucibles of growth, compassion and redemption.

Through many mistakes and wrong turns, they have found their way and created their own beautiful lives of grace and love and connection.

Only now can I honestly say that I am free. I am not lonely any more.

Acknowledgements

I acknowledge the unconditional love that my daughters have given me throughout the broken years of their childhood and their many trials and triumphs in adult life. They are my dearest friends, and paradoxically, by being torn apart, we have grown closer together. And though he is not part of this story, I acknowledge my son, who gave me a second chance at bringing up a child in love and loyalty and has been my anchor in the second half of my life.

The writing of this story began over twenty years ago and has had many reworkings and transformations. The last and most radical was after a structural edit by Sydney Smith. She taught me that conflict was the structuring principle of the narrative and, by stepping into my shoes while keeping her objective eye of reader/potential publisher, she coached me to discard many chapters and write many new ones. It was a painful process, and I'm glad it's finished, but Sydney, you are the best!

Many thanks to Danny Vendramini, patron of the Rosie Scott Writer's Studio, for the gift of week's writer's retreat in the Blue Mountains in 2020. The tranquil setting and clear atmosphere helped me focus on a difficult rewrite.

After the long gestation of this story, my heartfelt thanks to Ginninderra Press, that quiet, ethical, small publisher who helps so many authors get their work published with integrity and perfection. Thank you, Ginninderra!

Many other friends and writers and academics have encouraged and supported me along the way – Nicola-Jane le Breton, Maureen Helen, Elisabeth Hanscombe, Suzanne Covich, Marion May Campbell, Julienne van Loon, Mary Besemeres, Marian Edmunds, Maive Jackson-Colette, Sue Reynolds, Andrea Barton. Thank you all. May your own writing journeys be blessed.

The cover image is from an original painting of mine, *Footsteps in the Sand*.

The photo of my daughters on the back cover was taken soon after they were taken to America.

www.ingramcontent.com/pod-product-compliance
Lightning Source LLC
Chambersburg PA
CBHW020036120526
44589CB00031B/160